William Whittaker Barry

A Walking Tour in Normandy

William Whittaker Barry

A Walking Tour in Normandy

ISBN/EAN: 9783337327996

Printed in Europe, USA, Canada, Australia, Japan

Cover: Foto ©Andreas Hilbeck / pixelio.de

More available books at **www.hansebooks.com**

A WALKING TOUR

IN

NORMANDY.

BY THE AUTHOR OF
"ALL ROUND IRELAND ON FOOT."

Si quid novisti rectius istis,
Candidus imperti; si non, his utere mecum.
HORACE, Epis. Lib. I. 6.

LONDON:
RICHARD BENTLEY, NEW BURLINGTON STREET.
Publisher in Ordinary to Her Majesty.
1868.

R. BENTLEY AND CO., PRINTERS, LONDON.

PREFACE.

THE success which the "Walking Tour Round Ireland" attained, has induced me to write out and elaborate the journal of a similar course of travel in Normandy in 1863. I believe the circumstance that five years have since intervened will not diminish any value which the following pages may otherwise possess. The landscapes, cathedrals, and churches necessarily remain the same; and I think also that the hotels and country inns, and the mode of living generally, will, for the most part, be found to continue unchanged. I have not attempted to import into the present work any of that learning or historical lore which must be the result of much research and study at home. I have added a table of journies, stoppages, and distances for the special use of the pedestrian, and also to enable the general reader to form a practical idea of my progress through the country.

Many persons are deterred from travelling in Normandy through the idea that, before doing so, it is necessary to read up the Anglo-Norman history, and to master some work on church architecture. When that is done, they propose to themselves a visit to Normandy. But the exigencies of the profession or occupation at home demand all the attention; and besides, there is the natural disinclination to undertake a course of study as a preparation for a holiday tour. Hence from year to year the projected expedition is postponed, and the convenient season never arrives. Normandy is full of associations connected with England, and no doubt the traveller intimately acquainted with her early history would possess a great advantage in being able, wherever he trod, to wake the echoes of the past. The student of architecture must also feel a delight denied to others, when he inspects the cathedrals and churches of Normandy, and in doing so can realize the skill of the builders. But the main object of art is, by the general effect, to please the lay beholder, otherwise the work cannot be true to nature. For instance, the beautiful spire of the church of St. Pierre, at Caen, will rise up before the mental eye, in all its graceful proportions, years after it has been seen, and yet the visitor may not be able to give any technical description of the reason why it should gratify the beholder more than any ordinary church spire.

On the whole, I think that to postpone a visit to Normandy by reason of want of knowledge of history or architecture is a mistake. I may observe, however, that, to do the country justice, it should be made the subject of a distinct tour, and not merely the principal towns visited *en route* to or from Paris. With no other preparation than that stated in the opening chapter, I made my tour in Normandy, which proved thoroughly enjoyable in the present, and at intervals since has been the source of many agreeable and pleasant reminiscences. With no other aid in the shape of guide or handbook than this little work, I believe that the reader, if he so pleases, may, with pleasure and profit, do likewise. My book will certainly be found easy to carry, and I hope also it will prove light to read.

LONDON,
July, 1868.

CONTENTS.

PAGE

TABLE of Journies, Stoppages, and Distances xi

CHAPTER I.
London to Havre .... 1—18

CHAPTER II.
Honfleur—Chapel of Notre Dame—Departments of Normandy—Roads and distances—Vauderville—Trouville—The Hôtel de Paris—Bathing arrangements—Pont l'Evêque—The tribunal there—A wet walk—Reflections on travel—A regular down-pour—Beuzeville—Experiences at a country inn .... 19—41

CHAPTER III.
An old custom—A clean cap—Department of Eure—Villages of St. Maclon, Tontainville, and St. Germain—About the roads—Distance between Beuzeville and Pont Audemer—No English there—Description of the town—Banks of the Rille—Good fishing—Hôtel Pont d'Etain—Provincial brogue—Nature of Norman towns—Epaigues, Cormeilles, and Hermival—A short cut—Distance between Pont Audemer and Lisieux—Re-enter Calvados—Lisieux—Old streets—Cathedral—Church of St. Jacques—Gardens—Corbon—A halt—Distance between Lisieux and Caen—Reflections on the Conquest—Roadside inns—A spectral dog—A humble wish—Suburbs of Caen—The midnight hour—Enter the streets of Caen—Solitude of a great city—Search for the Hôtel d'Angleterre—A friendly guide—A modest wish, though not realized—To the rescue .... 42—59

CHAPTER IV.
A swarm of flies—Caen—Church of St. Pierre—St. Etienne, or Abbaye aux Hommes—Grave of the Conqueror—Reflections thereon—St. Etienne le Vieux—Abbaye aux Dames, or La Sainte Trinité—Church of St. Jean—St. Savern—Public school of the Lycée—Present appearance of Caen—Quays—Avenues of trees—Table d'hôte at Hôtel d'Angleterre—Set out for Bayeux—Village of Maladrerie—Quarries of stone—An old ruin—A lift—Bretteville—Bayeux—Hôtel du Luxembourg—The tapestry—Cathedral—A punctual host—Chapelle de Séminaire—Return to Caen—Church at Norrey—Caen again—Hôtel de Victoire—Place Royale—Hôtel de Ville—An uncivil porter—Philosophy from a little child—Com-

pulsory courtesy—A nondescript party—A welcome escape—A sumptuous repast—A hotel for the lover of good cheer... 60—79

CHAPTER V.

Wasps—Falaise—A holy calm, where to be found—Churches of St. Gervais and Ste. Trinité—An awkward predicament—A singular custom—Guibray—Castle of Falaise—Birthplace of William the Conqueror—Tradition of Arlotte—Tower of the castle—Exterior view—The Val d'Ante—Kissing among men—Statue to William the Conqueror—Hôtel de Normandie—Scenery of Calvados—A drunken landlord—Out of Calvados into Orne—Argentan—Écouché—Briouze—Flers—Tinchebray—Story of the battle—Re-enter Calvados—Vire—Church of Notre Dame—A coffin lying in state—Walks and castle—Hôtel St. Pierre—Fulfilment of a promise .... 80—98

CHAPTER VI.

Rich scenery—Torigny—A Sister of Mercy—Hôtel d'Augleterre—Interested fellow-travellers—St. Lo—Table d'hôte at Hôtel Soleil Levant—Brother Pedestrians—Description of town of St. Lo—Road to Coutances—Marigny—Coutances—Hôtel d'Angleterre again—The Cathedral—Church of St. Pierre—St. Nicholas—Public garden—Bréhal—Cider in a cup—A sale by auction—Dust—Granville—Hôtel du Nord—A wet day—Visit to the church—The lower town—General aspect of the place—A storm-signal—Sartilly—A courteous stranger—The valley of Sartilly—The return from market—Pont Callant—A delightful view—Avranches—Hôtel de France—Shut up in the public garden—My escape—A contrast .... 99—119

CHAPTER VII.

Avranches—Jardin des Plantes—Gateway of Chapel of St. George—Two churches—Museum—Court of Civil Tribunal—Stone, part of the old cathedral—A bath simple—The table d'hôte dinner—A new arrival—A profitable matter of inquiry—True French politeness—A deserted town—Fiction and travel—Village of Pont au Baud—Bad fare—A lift—Treacherous sands—Distant view of Mont St. Michel—A dangerous ford—Mont St. Michel—An indolent guide—Reception at the castle—The cloisters—Church—Dining-hall—Dungeons—A military salute—The workrooms—Dormitories—College and council chamber—The last to leave—Road to Pont d'Orson—Its wretched condition—A good-natured driver—Large families—Pont d'Orson—The church—Distance from Avranches—Hôtel de la Poste—A comfortable café—A literary girl .... 120—136

CHAPTER VIII.

A simple inscription—St. James—A funeral service—Hôtel St. Jacques—A case for sympathy—A cloth mill—St. Hilaire du Harcouet—The church there—Hôtel de la Croix Blanche—A liberal host—Mortain—Hôtel de la Poste—A severe rebuke—The cascades—The church—Voitures—Barenton—Out of Manche into Orne—A lift—An unexpected host—Domfront—Juvigny—Fairday—A whirligig—A crowded inn—A new custom—A regular downpour—Villages of La Chapelle—Moche and Couterne—Enter department of Mayenne—Couptrain—An inhospitable inn—A ready mode of exit—Remarks on treatment of strangers—A walk by moonlight—Prez-en-Pail—Moderate charges—Suggestion to the pedestrian—Distance... 137—154

CHAPTER IX.

A fine village church—Wayside crosses—Out of Mayenne into Orne—St. Denis—Entrance to Alençon—A band playing—The cathedral—Hôtel Grand Cerf—Table d'hôte dinner there—Comments on travel—The public promenade—Cathedral again—Museum—Public library—Other buildings—A lift—Le Ménil Broux—An independent innkeeper—Le Mesle-sur-Sarthe—Mortagne-sur-Huine—The church—Hôtel de la Bouille—An uncivil landlady—A humble table d'hôte—A pretty but useless waiting-maid—A stroll after dinner—Mode of checking incivility at inns—St. Maurice—Out of Orne and re-enter Eure—Verneuil—Hôtel de la Poste—Passports...155—170

CHAPTER X.

Verneuil—The church of the convent—Nuns at service—Reflections on their mode of life—The church of Notre Dame—St. Laurent—La Tour Grise—A jovial Miller—Church of l'Hobital—The Madeleine—St. Jean—Place de la Madeleine—A cracked basin—An unpleasant departure—Breteuil—An unfrequented road—A cunning dog—A poacher—A wild country—The forest of Evreux—Twilight—Reach Evreux—Hôtel du Grand Cerf—Full of guests—Bad accommodation—A primitive ball-room—The cathedral—The bishop's garden—The palace—The bishop at prayers—The cloisters—Church of St. Taurin—Public buildings—Picturesque villages—Louviers—A very pretty girl—Hôtel du Mouton......... 171—186

B

CHAPTER XI.

Louviers—Church of Notre Dame—Maison des Templiers—Out of Eure into Seine Inférieure—Caudebec—Elbeuf—The churches of St. Jean and St. Etienne—Orival; the chapel there—A route little traversed—A cart without springs—Grand Couron—A friendly Frenchman—An unromantic word—A dark walk—A lost cat—The suburbs of Rouen—Suggested route through the forest—Rouen—Politeness at a café—The Hôtel d'Angleterre—The cathedral—Church of St. Maclou—St. Ouen—Public gardens—Library—Gallery of paintings—Museum—Palais de Justice—Other public buildings—Church of St. Vincent—General description of Rouen—An earthquake on the spot—An excellent hotel...... 187—199

CHAPTER XII.

Reasons for detaining the attention of the reader—Nature of the scenery—Climate—Church architecture—Closing the country churches—Desecration of old churches—Middle-class worshippers—Absence of wayside crosses—Public gardens—Modes of travelling—Passports—French money—The country inns—Cider—Vin ordinaire—Melons—Tripe—Cleanliness of the beds—Expense of living—Company at the inns—Mode of salutation—Cafés—Absence of drunkenness—Manners of the Normans—The gentry—Their houses—Flax-spinning—Playing at bowls—Expressions of the peasantry—Personal appearance of the Normans—Beauty of the women—Their bad taste in dress .... 200—230

CHAPTER XIII.

A road under repair—Maromme—Malaunay—No scenery—Tôtes—Good walking condition—The church at Tôtes—The inn—Reception there—An indigestible dinner—A civil commercial gentleman—Again no scenery—The approach to Dieppe—End of my long journey—My claim to sympathy—Reach Dieppe—Weatherworn—Reception at the Hôtel Victoria—Hôtel d'Angleterre—The church—A querulous American—Castle and shops—General description of Dieppe—Early to bed—A dream—Process of calling—Leave Dieppe—Fine passage—Party of Germans—About clean linen—English spoken, but not understood—Reach Newhaven—An uncivil gatekeeper—An appropriate resting-place—Reflections on the past—Journey to London .... 231—249

INDEX 251

TABLE OF JOURNIES, STOPPAGES, AND DISTANCES.

1863.
AUGUST.

Sunday, 30th.	Left London.
Monday, 31st.	Reached Havre.

SEPTEMBER.

		Fr. K.	En. M.
Tuesday, 1st, and Wednesday, 2nd.	Havre.		
Thursday, 3rd.	Havre to Honfleur.		
Friday, 4th.	Honfleur to Trouville	14	9
Saturday, 5th.	Trouville to Beuzeville	25	15
Sunday, 6th.	Beuzeville to Pont Audemer	16	10
Monday, 7th.	Pont Audemer to Lisieux	36	22
Tuesday, 8th.	Lisieux to Caen	48	29
Wednesday, 9th.	Caen.		
Thursday, 10th.	Caen to Bayeux	27	17
Friday, 11th.	Bayeux to Caen	27	17
Saturday, 12th.	Caen to Falaise	34	21
Sunday, 13th.	Falaise.		
Monday, 14th.	Falaise to Argentan.	22	13
Tuesday, 15th.	Argentan to Flers	43	26
Wednesday, 16th.	Flers to Vire	30	18
Thursday, 17th.	Vire to Torigny	25	15
Friday, 18th.	Torigny to Coutances	42	26
		389	238

TABLE OF JOURNIES, ETC.

		Fr. K.	En. M.
SEPTEMBER.	Brought forward .	389	238
Saturday, 19th.	Coutances to Granville. .	29	18
Sunday, 20th.	Granville.		
Monday, 21st.	Granville to Avranches .	26	16
Tuesday, 22nd.	Avranches.		
Wednesday, 23rd.	Avranches to Pont d'Orson	22	13
Thursday, 24th.	Pont d'Orson to St. Hilaire du Harcouet	35	21
Friday, 25th.	St. Hilaire du Harcouet to Domfront.	40	24
Saturday, 26th.	Domfront to Prez-en-Pail .	40	24
Sunday, 27th.	Prez-en-Pail to Alençon .	23	14
Monday, 28th.	Alençon.		
Tuesday, 29th.	Alençon to Mortagne-sur-Huine	39	23
Wednesday, 30th.	Mortagne to Verneuil . .	38	22
OCTOBER.			
Thursday, 1st.	Verneuil to Evreux . . .	40	24
Friday, 2nd.	Evreux to Louviers . . .	22	13
Saturday, 3rd.	Louviers to Rouen . . .	38	22
Sunday, 4th.	Rouen.		
Monday, 5th.	Rouen to Tôtes . .	29	18
Tuesday, 6th.	Tôtes to Dieppe	29	18
Wednesday, 7th.	Dieppe to London.		
		839	508

A WALKING TOUR IN NORMANDY.

CHAPTER I.

London to Havre.

A WALKING tour in Brittany, in the autumn of the year 1860, suggested the idea that a similar expedition to Normandy some day or other would prove a more agreeable and interesting excursion. Accordingly, in the month of August of the year 1863, I determined to carry out my holiday project. As some preparation for the journey, I read the modern works of travel about Normandy which I could find. These were only two; one by Mr. Musgrave, a clergyman of Devonshire, who styles his book "A Ramble in Normandy," but in fact it is confined entirely to the department of Calvados. The work, however, is very interesting, and gives an elaborate account of Caen, Bayeux and its tapestry, Falaise, Lisieux, and one or two other places. The reverend writer also has entered with spirit into the *genius loci,* having collected from historical sources all about the life and times of the Conqueror, which, read in connection with the places visited, always proves instructive, however old and hackneyed the information may be. The other work to which I allude is "Life in Normandy," an anonymous book, in two goodly tomes, but which it has transpired is written by Walter Campbell, of Islay, a deceased Scotch gentleman of great estate and wealth; but becoming impoverished, chiefly through the liberal manner in which he endeavoured to alleviate the distresses of his poor neighbours during a period of calamity, he became an outcast from his country, and settled in Normandy, at Avranches. Here Mr. Campbell dwelt during the remainder of his life, and carried with him to the new country those sporting tastes which he had been accustomed to cultivate in his native land. The book takes the form of imaginary conversations, in the course of which the modes of fishing, shooting, and sporting in Normandy are fully described, with the assistance of some truly excellent plates. There is much in the work about the scenes and events of the French revolution of 1848 which might have been very advantageously omitted; but, on the whole, it is full of that kind of local information which none but the resident of years in a place can hope to obtain. It is always interesting, I think, to read a little beforehand with reference to the country one may propose to visit. By these means the traveller is prepared what to look for and expect, and how best to economize his time and money. With such view I sit down to write an account of my five weeks' travel in Normandy, which I hope may serve as a kind of *avant-coureur* to such of my readers who may at any time propose to visit that country, and also, I trust, prove interesting to those who intend to remain at home. But my object will be, not to copy elaborate and technical descriptions from books, of cathedrals, churches, and places which I visited, but to give a plain, truthful, and original account of what I saw and did, and of the lions and localities as they appeared to your humble servant the writer, and no other.

Without further comments, then, I come to the commencement of my travels, which began on the 30th of August, 1863. Early in the morning of that day—which was a Sunday—lightly clothed, and with an umbrella and a knapsack not too heavily filled, I started from my bachelor quarters on foot for St. Katherine's Wharf, in order to take the boat for Havre. The few passengers who were going by her were punctual in attendance, but she lay long past the hour appointed for departure, fast stuck in the mud on the other side of the river, and so we had to wait the pleasure of the tide before moving onward. There is something peculiarly unpleasant in a sudden check at the commencement, even of a journey of idleness and pleasure. It is not at all agreeable to rise early, breakfast in a hurry, and rush to the place of embarcation, and yet by noon find yourself not advanced a stage. There is something in your express trains, after all. Heigh ho! John, Thomas, James! pack up my small portmanteau, and fetch a hansom. To London Bridge, into a comfortable first-class carriage, and before I can dismiss thoughts of home, I am at Folkestone; in sight of the sea, at least, and with only two hours' passage between me and La Belle France. But I promised not to give reins to the imagination, but to confine myself to my own humble travels, and yet I am rambling away already. Oh, how easy to form resolutions, and yet how difficult to keep them!

So I return from this digression to the wharf where I stand, seeing the interesting process going forward of dragging unwilling oxen ashore from the hold of the steamer alongside. After a while the Havre boat made its appearance, looking by no means cleanly or inviting. She had anything but her Sunday clothes on, and I fancied the expectant passengers seemed rather glum at sight of her. The effect, at all events as regards myself, was particularly disappointing; for, having several times been taken in by steamboats before, I took the precaution to go to the wharf a week previously, to make inquiries, when I was informed by a most respectable-looking man that she was lying on the other side of the river, but I should be throwing away a shilling to go on board, as she was just like that there—

pointing to a much superior-looking vessel alongside. As the Havre boat is nearing towards me, therefore, I arrive at the charitable conclusion that it would be wise never again to trust to the word of any one about the docks. And here I am reminded of a bargain I once made with a porter at these same docks, who had evidently mistaken his vocation, or he would have been bred to the Bar. I agreed that for so much he should carry my luggage from the cab to the steamboat. Nothing, apparently, could be more free from ambiguity; but on reaching the vessel he demanded some further payment. "Why," said I, "surely we agreed plain enough?"

"Begging your pardon, sir," the man replied, "I agreed to take the luggage *to* the vessel; but this is *on* the vessel."

The argument, though technical, I felt to be unanswerable.

However, I had come to the wharf, and was not now for going back; so I crossed the steamer, called, I think, the "Baron Osy," and got on board the Havre boat which was outside, and the name whereof does not stand recorded either in my notes or my memory. And I do not regret the circumstance, for I have no wish that the reader, for his own comfort sake, should make her acquaintance. I envy, as I pass, the superior cleanliness of the "Baron Osy," bound on her last voyage to Antwerp, for she was wrecked on her return somewhere near the mouth of the Thames. At last, at 11·30 A.M., we are fairly under weigh, and taking camp stools from the cabin we remained on deck until, at an early hour, dinner is announced, of which we all partook, for there were, as yet, no symptoms of sea-sickness on board. The weather remained beautifully clear and fine throughout the voyage, which was a fortunate circumstance for myself, as I was ultimately dreadfully ill, and had to be on deck nearly all the night. Towards morning the sea, which had been gradually rising, became very rough, and I was frequently washed by the spray. Nearly all were more or less sick. About the only exception was that of a well-known author on board (now, alas! dead), who bore the sea like any sailor without flinching. And thus the voyage, which promised to be so calm and pleasant, turned out, to use the trustworthy term of the engine-man, "a dirty passage." At length, about noon on Monday, the 31st August, to our great joy we sighted the coast near Havre, and there seemed some hope of being shortly landed. The sea had become more calm, and the sun was shining beautifully. But now it was discovered by our worthy captain, with an appearance of the most innocent surprise, that partly by reason of the late departure from St. Katherine's Wharf, and partly owing to the rough passage, we should not be able to get into the harbour this tide, but must wait until the next, at 11 P.M. Such a thing had not occurred for thirty, forty, or I don't know how many voyages. It was a most rare occurrence. I always think, however, that there is little consolation to be derived from the idea that yours is an exceptional case and something quite apart from the general rule.

There was a curious coincidence between the dinner-hour on board and the time when we ought to, or might have been entering the harbour. This circumstance led my mind into uncharitable speculations on the subject. How about the meals? Are they provided by the captain and steward? and if so, does the profit belong as a perquisite to them? And have they any temptation, therefore, to prolong the voyage? But I never feel inclined to grumble travelling, without being reminded of the celebrated passage in Sterne's "Sentimental Journey," about the traveller—the learned Smellfungus, supposed to be a sly hit at Smollett—who had been half over the continent without finding anything to his liking, but only a succession of annoyances. "'I will tell it,' says he, 'to the world.' 'You had better tell it to your physician,' said I." So I have no doubt my uncharitable thoughts on this occasion were owing to the bile—though what that means I have never the least idea—or to the sea-sickness, which is much more intelligible. However, it being clear as a fact, whatever the cause, that we were too late to enter the harbour, the captain, in order to relieve the monotony of remaining still, put out to sea again for two or three hours, and then we returned and anchored opposite to Cap de la Hève, where, until eleven o'clock, we enjoyed that peculiar kind of oscillating movement which always proves so delightful to those who suffer from sea-sickness. At that hour we weighed anchor, and in a short time were in the harbour. Here occurred those numerous loud and vociferous directions on the part of the captain, such as "Turn her astern;" "Let go that rope;" "Make room, will you?" "What the deuce are you about there?" "Gently;" "Easy;" "Make fast," etc., etc., without which it does not appear constitutional for a vessel ever to enter any harbour or dock. Though when a steamboat performs the same voyage two or three times every week, I am surprised that the same difficulties should occur over and over again. In this instance several small vessels had comfortably housed themselves for the night exactly where we designed, and had apparently the right to be. This was enough to provoke a saint, and our captain was not sparing in his observations on the proceeding. By degrees those on board the vessels were roused and made to understand that they must find quarters somewhere else, which they proceeded slowly to do, and we were moored alongside the wharf.

It was now midnight, and most of the passengers had turned into their berths for the night; but several of them, including myself, were only too glad to get ashore. It was dark, and I had never been to Havre before; but with some difficulty I found my way to the Hôtel Frascati, which I selected, as it was the first on Murray's list, and near the sea. But there was no living being moving there, and I could see no light. The whole hotel seemed nestled in repose. I rang a bell, but it evidently sounded as if in some out quarter, as I discovered, on inspecting the premises next day, must have been the case. At all events, no one answered the bell, so I was obliged to make my way back to the principal quay, along which I had passed, and there I discovered the Hôtel de l'Amirauté. The bell rang loud and clear, and soon brought the night porter, who showed me to a small bedroom on one of the upper floors, where I was quickly in bed and asleep.

I rose late on the morning of Tuesday, the 1st of September, and having breakfasted, walked out to see the place. I was agreeably disappointed with the general appearance of Havre. I had formed an impression—I know not how—that it was a dirty seaport kind of looking town; but, in point of fact, it has many agreeable features. I walked down the principal street, which is called the Rue de Paris.

This is a fine street, and has some good shops. To the right, about half way down, is the Church of Notre Dame, a large plain edifice, but without containing anything particularly deserving of notice. Around it is an inclosure with trees and seats, proving, no doubt, an agreeable retreat for the inhabitants of the crowded street. At the bottom of the Rue de Paris is the Hôtel de Ville, a fine building, with a garden attached, which is very prettily laid out. On my way back I went into two or three shops in order to obtain a map of Normandy, a most indispensable article for the pedestrian traveller. I at first feared I should fail in obtaining it, for though at two places they had plenty of plans of Havre, they had no map of the country generally. At last, however, I found, at a corner shop near the square, a very good map of Normandy, without which I should have been very much in the position of the sailor without his compass. I may here observe that my attention was directed to a French "Guide to Normandy," by E. Tasser, which I think might prove useful, though I did not obtain it myself, being already provided with "Murray's Handbook."

Having changed some English coins into French money, in order to rid myself of loose cash, for I had already obtained some Napoleons in London, I made my way to the bathing-place at the Hôtel Frascati, for the purpose of having a plunge in the sea. The dressing-boxes are up on the beach, and not movable like our English bathing-machines, but fixed; and they are accessible to any thief who might be prowling about in search of prey. I must say I did not much like the idea of leaving my purse there, so, for prudence sake, I put it in one of my boots, over which I placed a sock, thinking that probably no thief would look for money in such a quarter, but not finding the purse in any of the usual depositaries, would suppose that the traveller had left it at his hotel. I adopted a like course with reference to my watch, which I placed in a similar manner in the other boot.

The bathing here is pretty good, but shingly. You are provided—of course I am speaking of the gentlemen, for of the mysteries of the ladies' department I know nothing—with a pair of short drawers, and enveloped in a kind of white sheet fitting loosely, and looking very much like a ghost, you proceed to the shore, where you may divest yourself of the latter garment, and leave it on the beach or some rails there before going into the sea. On returning to the dressing-box, the attendant provides you with a pail of warm water for the feet, which is a great luxury. The price of the bath is half a franc, to which should be added ten cents for a towel, ten cents for the hot water, and ten cents for the attendant, making together eighty cents. But you may subscribe, as in England. There are other bathing-places along the beach, but none so good as that at the Hôtel Frascati.

I afterwards walked on the North Pier, or jetty, which forms a very good promenade. I think that from here you obtain the best general view of the town and port of Havre. Standing at the end of the pier, looking seaward to the left, you have a good view of the coast of Normandy, presenting the appearance of a narrow strip of land very much like an island; and to the right you see the pretty village of Saint Adresse, and further on the promontory and lighthouses of Cap de la Hève; and looking inland you obtain a good general view of the town of Havre, with its quays and shipping. I then returned to the hotel to the *table d'hôte* dinner, which was good, well served, and moderately attended. Then out again on the pier for that evening stroll which is always so refreshing at the sea-side, and back to coffee and an early bed.

The next day (Wednesday, September 2nd) I walked down the Rue de Paris, past the Hôtel de Ville, and on up some steps to the hill above the suburb of Ingouville. From a field here you command a good bird's-eye view of the town and port of Havre, but not so picturesque or pleasing, I think, as the scene from the pier. This information will, no doubt, prove serviceable to those who from any reason do not feel disposed to ascend a hill. From this spot I walked some distance into the country, which, however, beyond becomes flat and uninteresting enough. Then I retraced my steps, and proceeded over the cliffs to the village of Saint Adresse, which is romantically situated in a valley, with a pretty little church. There are a good many nice suburban residences here which look delightfully charming and rural. Altogether it is quite a lovely spot, though, as I am just escaped from the centre of London, perhaps my praises may be too rapturous, and so the reader had better accept my statement *cum grano salis*, as the Latinists say. From the village of Saint Adresse the obvious course is to do as I did, namely, walk on to the lighthouses at Cap de la Hève. From the number of French ladies and gentlemen I observed walking in this direction, I imagine it to be a popular excursion; and truly it is pleasant to escape from the town, and find oneself treading soft turf instead of hard pavement. About halfway to the lighthouses there is a small chapel, intended, I presume, not so much for sailors, since few of them are likely to ascend so far, as for the purpose of offering up prayers on behalf of those whose business takes them on the great waters. Returning by the beach, I reached the hotel in time for the *table d'hôte*.

At breakfast this morning (Thursday, September 3rd) there is seated opposite to me a young English married couple, indulging in that light small talk which no doubt forms such an agreeable feature of the honeymoon, and apparently unconscious of my near propinquity; or perhaps they take me for a Frenchman (as my moustache is already full grown) who does not understand their language. But I will not report the conversation, though it led to some philosophical mental comments; and, alas! I fancy I discover already the elements of disunion, but which Heaven prevent!

So to divert my mind from this melancholy reflection I turn to observe a family group just entering the *salle à manger* — Paterfamilias travelling *en suite*. "Are those twins?" I ask of the young girl near me. "Oh dear no, sir," she replies, as if amazed. There was, no doubt, the usual interval of twelve months or so between the arrival of these innocents in the nursery, and to suppose therefore that they came into the world together seemed to disconcert the ideas of the little maid. Being therefore on the wrong track for conversation, I feel compelled to beat a retreat, and to bury myself in Murray until it is time to pay the bill and start for Honfleur.

Before leaving Havre, however, I would recommend the reader who visits this place not to come direct from London, but by way of Southampton. The passage money will be a little more, but the boats are better and the sea-voyage shorter. For the sake also of those who do not like moving about, I would observe that Havre will be found excellent head-quarters for making excursions. You may visit by day trips Harfleur, Honfleur, the pretty watering-place of Trouville, and go up the Seine to Rouen.

CHAPTER II.

Honfleur—Chapel of Notre Dame—Departments of Normandy— Roads and distances—Vauderville—Trouville—The Hôtel de Paris—Bathing arrangements—Pont l'Evêque—The tribunal there—A wet walk—Reflections on travel—A regular downpour—Beuzeville—Experiences at a country inn.

Thursday, Sept. 3rd (continued). — About eleven o'clock this morning I left by the steamboat, which starts from the quay opposite the hotel, for Honfleur. The vessel has a pleasant awning overhead, which is welcome enough as the sun is warm. Altogether the boat presents a striking contrast to that I had come by from London, and shows a more civilized aspect. I am always struck with the difference between the Channel steamers and those traversing pleasure routes like the present in "get up," cleanliness, comfort, and attention. I presume the reason to be that the directors or managers feel that persons *must* cross the Channel however ugly the means of transport may look, but they need not go on rivers, lakes, and the like, and therefore you must afford some temptation in the way of a superior boat with internal arrangements to match.

It was a pleasant sail across the bay of the Seine to Honfleur, the weather very fine, and the sea, if it may be called so here, smooth. On arriving at Honfleur I put up at the Hôtel Angleterre and Cheval Blanc, formerly two inns, but now converted into one and the same. Honfleur is a busy mercantile kind of place, wearing a most working appearance. The inn is full of captains and others, evidently of sea-faring occupations, and it is clear that I am already passing away from beyond the beaten track of the tourist. Indeed, in order to escape from a scene so alien to my present feelings, I shortly leave the hotel and take what appears to be the one great walk at Honfleur. A winding hilly path, with here and there good views over the town and suburbs below, leads to the small votive chapel of Notre Dame, situate on an eminence overlooking the Seine. The chapel contains many pictures, showing, in rude outlines, hair-breadth escapes from shipwreck at sea, and thereby evincing the thankfulness to Providence for their well-nigh miraculous preservation. I like the idea, though of course it savours of superstition. It certainly tends to show that the sailor mind is not so careless and oblivious as people are generally prone to imagine.

From this eminence there is a very fine view over the Seine, with Harfleur on the opposite shore. There is a building here which you can enter on payment of a trifle, where are some curiosities, and you can assist the naked eye if you please by the aid of a telescope. I then walked down again into the town, and saw the two churches. One of these is made of wood, and well worthy of inspection. Close adjoining to it there is a curious old tower, serving as a kind of market-place. The *table d'hôte* dinner at the inn was good and well served. A business air pervaded the guests, none of whom, so far as I could make out, were bent on pleasure. I observed on the eminence some English gentlemen who had come over by the boat from Havre, but evidently merely for the day, having returned by the evening steamer.

For the information of those of my readers who may not be well acquainted with the geography of France, I may observe that Normandy consists of five departments, namely, Seine Inférieure, Calvados, Eure, Orne, and Manche. Havre, my starting-point, is in Seine Inférieure; but on crossing the bay of the Seine I enter, at Honfleur, the department of Calvados.

Before I take the reader with me on my first walking journey in Normandy, I must say something about the roads he will meet with, and the way in which the distances are measured. There are three kinds of roads in France; first, the Route Imperial or Royal—the dynasties in this country change so rapidly, that you will sometimes find one and sometimes another on a sign-post—which is a very good and wide road, along which such diligences as remain pass for the most part, and about two or three times as broad as our turnpike roads in England. Then, secondly, there is the Route Departmental, which is also a good road, but not so broad as the other by about a half. It resembles very much a good ordinary turnpike-road in England. Then, thirdly, there is the Route of Grand Communication, answering very much to our by-roads in England, though kept in much better order. Indeed, most of them are about the width, and as well maintained as the roads through the grounds to an English country gentleman's mansion. The distances are measured in kilomètres and mètres. A mètre is equal to about—being rather more than—three English feet. A thousand mètres go to one kilomètre, which is little more than a half of an English mile. For all practical purposes five kilomètres are equal to three English miles. In the course of my journeys I shall give the distances first in French kilomètres and then approximately in English miles. At all the principal cross-roads will be found clearly painted sign-posts, giving the distance to the towns and principal villages along the roads there, and with arrows pointing out the direction. In every town, village, and even hamlet, on the walls of some house there is a plate giving the name of the place and the distance to the towns and villages. In the villages and hamlets only one of these plates will be met with, that being enough, but in the towns you will find a plate on some wall of a house near each of the roads leading out of the place. These sign-posts and direction-plates are of inestimable advantage to the pedestrian traveller in France. I rarely had occasion to ask my way, and never the name of a place. Most persons who have walked at all in England must have experienced the inconvenience of having to ask the name of some village they happen to be passing through. How the children laugh and titter, and the grown-up people grin, as if you were asking some silly question you ought as a matter of course to know. Though I often wonder, and sometimes feel inclined to ask how, in the name of common sense, a stranger is, without inquiry, to discover the name of a village which he enters for the first time in his life? After the care taken of the traveller in France as regards sign-posts, it is perhaps hardly necessary to remark that kilomètre stones are placed along all the roads. Only on two or three occasions did I miss the direction I wished to take, and that merely for a very short distance.

Friday, Sept. 4th.—I feel sure that the reader who may be disposed to follow my footsteps through Normandy will benefit by the foregoing description of the roads there, and that the stay-at-home reader will forgive my pausing a moment to act the part of an itinerary. But now I pursue my daily chronicle. I am reminded early this morning that I am at a seafaring place, for at four o'clock I am awoke by those numerous objurgations and noises incidental to the moving of a vessel. I remember observing, the evening before, lying on the mud, nearly opposite the hotel, a small schooner of about two hundred tons burden, and now with the morning tide her crew are removing her from her moorings. After breakfast I leave *en route* for Trouville, distant from Honfleur fourteen kilomètres (or nine English miles). The road proceeds for the most part along the shore of the bay, and is pretty and interesting. I pass through Vauderville, a large village with a good hotel apparently, by the sea-side. This is a quiet retired spot, well suited for those who prefer solitude to the noise and bustle of Trouville, and it is no doubt a more economical resting-place. It forms a walk for the visitors at Trouville to come here, as I meet many fashionable-looking people on their way out to-day.

I reach Trouville about mid-day. I put up at the Hôtel de Paris, a very large establishment, and without doubt the best inn here; indeed, there is no other of at all equal size or pretensions. It is, however, very dear, my bedroom being charged five francs. It was, though, a good-sized chamber with a curtain to hide the bed, and suitable, if necessary, for a sitting-room as well. But the situation was unfortunate; it overlooked the stables, and the night-air brought a most unpleasant odour from that quarter, so that the most humble bed at a wayside inn would have proved much more welcome. There are some persons—indeed I frequently meet such, especially ladies—who on hearing any such complaint, remark placidly, "Oh, of course, a pedestrian must expect these things," or "put up with such things," as if he should rather enjoy them than otherwise, or were more impervious than others; but this is a mistake. Walking continually in the open air renders a person much more sensitive to any of the unpleasant smells about hotels than one who has been travelling all day in stuffy first-class railway-carriages. No royal changes of raiment can equal in cleanliness nature's drenching rain, followed by sunshine and a drying wind. However, with the exception of the locality of the bedroom, the Hôtel de Paris proved a first-rate establishment in its *table d'hâte* and general arrangements.

Trouville is a small town prettily situated on a gentle eminence above the sea-side. It has become one of the most fashionable watering-places in France. It is also much frequented by the English, about a thousand, I was informed, having come here this season. The sands are very fine, as good or better than at Ramsgate. You see here the bathing going forward according to the genuine French system. It was a fine afternoon, with the exception of two or three showers, and the scene on the sands between one and four o'clock was one of great animation and excitement. There are three divisions for bathing purposes, separated the one from the other by ropes supported on poles, which are removed as soon as the time allotted to bathing has passed, so as not to interfere with the promenade along the sands. The division to the left is appropriated to the ladies alone, who, however, bathe here in full bathing-dresses; that to the right is reserved for gentlemen alone, using simply short drawers; that in the centre is for ladies and gentlemen who choose to bathe together, but of course in this division both the sexes are equipped in complete bathing-dresses. In the ladies' divisions male attendants of sturdy aspect take them out and perform the duties of guiding and dipping. The guiding, indeed, does not involve much trouble, as the young ladies rarely venture out beyond knee-deep. The dipping is performed in a most peculiar fashion, such as would astonish and annoy English girls at our watering-places. The male attendant has a small bucket which he fills with water, and then souses it over the young lady's head, while she screams during the process. The dress of the ladies and gentlemen presents a very similar appearance, though no doubt on a nearer inspection some differences of detail would be disclosed. It consists of an elegant-looking garment, coloured, and fitting rather loosely, but close enough to show the figure, and coming down below the knee. The hair of the ladies is tied up, and evidently arranged with extreme care. Two or three girls will join hands with one another, or with two or three gentlemen, and skip together in a frolicsome kind of way to the sea. Indeed, this short promenade from the dressing-boxes to the waves is evidently one of the principal features of our neighbours' system of bathing. It enables the company to see and be seen in a state of demi-toilette. A French comic paper had a sketch of a gentleman wishing to form an acquaintance with a young lady, offering to escort her under an umbrella to the sea. I thought this showed that the French themselves considered that beneath their system of bathing there lurked a good deal of what we in England vulgarly call "humbug."

In the gentlemen's division there were two or three small one-oar kind of boats at hand, for those who like to paddle about while bathing. There was also a large boat to take out to sea those sensible men who wished to have a swim *au naturel* far away. The bathing looked very good, though I had been so much engaged in watching, and so puzzled at first with the regulations, that I allowed the time to pass away without a bathe. These complicated arrangements are very perplexing to the stranger, who may, innocently enough, contravene some well-established rule of the place, by bathing a few yards to the right or left of his proper position.

I observed no actual impropriety, though here and there a gentleman in the toilet of a savage would be speaking to some ladies who approached the rope, and who might have been his wife and other near relatives, though the sight appeared very unseemly. One thing, also, I remarked—that, though English ladies and girls were about the sands, looking on at the strange scene before them with peering and modest eyes, yet none of them appeared to be bathing. And yet I presume that French ladies would hardly like to venture into the sea in English fashion. How singular these customs seem to the philosophic observer of the manners of different countries. On the whole, however, I prefer the English system of bathing at the sea-side. "An excess of delicacy is indelicacy." Indeed, I think there could not be devised a mode of undress less attractive than that adopted by English ladies at the sea-side. I have frequently seen pretty girls at our watering-places walking along the sands, or over the shingly beach, with dishevelled hair; or more sedately over the cliffs, or along the esplanade; or promenading on the turf to the playing of the band; or eating sweets in a pastrycook's shop; or on horseback; but, though I confess to being a moderate observer—not a starer, mind—of English young ladies bathing, I never yet saw a pretty girl in the water. Nor are their movements either graceful or becoming—as, indeed, there is no reason why they should be, for they are supposed to be enjoying the healthful recreation of bathing, far removed from the sight of the male sex. Indeed, I can imagine some faded old maid, in days of yore, collecting around her all the young and beautiful girls of her acquaintance, and, after descanting in eloquent language on the way in which those vulgar men stared, proposing the adoption of the present loose black gown as the best artifice for resisting the languid look of the impressionable, or the steady gaze of the lascivious. There is, however some room for improvement in the regulations for bathing at our watering-places. I have occasionally been told by a young lady that during the past season she has learnt to swim, though how she managed to do so with the present kind of garment I never ventured to ask. There should be a tight-fitting robe, which would enable girls easily to acquire the useful art of swimming. Moreover, I feel sure that some of those mysterious cases of drowning of men reputed strong swimmers, and attributed to cramp, are more likely caused by the impediment occasioned by those loosely-fitting drawers prescribed by the custom of the place. A light garment, such as is worn by the athlete, would be safer to the wearer, and answer better the purposes of propriety. Then the sexes should be more widely separated, and not placed *vis-à-vis*, as at present. With such changes and modifications, I think our system of bathing would be as near perfection as possible with reference to a pastime from which a certain delicacy of feeling and sentiment is necessarily inseparable.

While these thoughts are filling my mind, the bathers are becoming fewer and fewer, and the period allowed being over, the ropes are removed, and the sands left free for the promenaders. These, however, are no longer many now the principal sight of the day is over. Only those are left who really enjoy a walk by the sea waves, or the delicate who remain for constitutional purposes. The steamer is just leaving on its return journey to Havre, and this takes away a certain number of the visitors. There is a large, rough, wooden tent near the shore, for those to take refuge in when caught by one of those frequent short showers which are so common in Normandy, and which I make acquaintance with for the first time to-day, and of which I shall have more to say by and by. In the evening I walked a good deal along the sands, but there were few people about promenading at the sea-side at this time—such a practice being evidently not so common a diversion with the French as at English watering-places. However, there is no band here to enliven the scene.

Saturday, Sept. 5th.—I walked down to the sands this morning before breakfast, in order to bathe if practicable, but all the dressing-boxes were deserted, and no attendant was there, so I had to give up the idea. I thought the aspect of the bathing arrangements this morning showed clearly enough that the French only resort to such pastime as a fashionable lounge, and not as a quiet recreation or means of healthful enjoyment. After breakfast I started on my journey to Pont l'Evêque, which is distant from Trouville about eleven kilomètres (or seven miles), though, through some unaccountable reason, I do not find the exact distance down on my notes. The road from Trouville to Pont l'Evêque is very dull, with no scenery. Pont l'Evêque is an old and interesting town. I entered the tribunal, which was now holding its sittings here, *de correction en la première instance.* Three judges, or magistrates, were sitting on the bench, and in a box by the side was another functionary, who put in a word now and then, and I presume, therefore, was the public prosecutor. The court-house, which was very commodious, was crowded with common people, to hear the last cause on the list, evidently one of interest, and no doubt reserved until then on account of the undue proportion of time it would occupy. The case was this :—The youth in the dock had been guilty of some insubordination towards his mistress, who was the prosecutrix; nothing very grave—absence and inattention to work, and rude answers. The servant was defended by an advocate who spoke at some length and with great energy, and some eloquence, and with a good deal of gesticulation. He was a young man, and I should hope will some day exercise his talents in a wider sphere, and become distinguished at the Paris bar. At present he is evidently well known along the country side, and from the rapt attention of the audience, it is no doubt his speech which they have come to hear, though not openly to applaud; for I was struck with the proceedings throughout, which were most orderly and regular. The only witness was the mistress. The servant was examined most kindly by the president, and a little by the functionary in the side box. The prisoner was allowed to have his say without any interruption.

When the case had been fully heard, the president opened a book of the code, and read the article applicable to the case, which empowered him to award a punishment of three or six months' imprisonment. He then commented on the nature of the offence, and pointed out to the youth how seriously it would interfere with his future prospects in life if the court inflicted the punishment authorized by the law. After a few other remarks of a similar nature, the president said that as this was a first offence, he should discharge the prisoner with a reprimand.

This decision of the tribunal seemed to give general satisfaction to the assembled crowd. It was firm and yet kind. No punishment was actually inflicted, and yet one seemed to be awarded; though the judge could not be more gentle had he been a master in his own parlour reprimanding a favourite servant for some slight fault, but whom he wished to retain in his service. That youth must possess a heart of stone and a mind of flint if this lesson conveyed to him by an impartial judge, in the presence of relatives, friends, acquaintances, and strangers, does not materially influence for good his future career in life.

Thus the last case being disposed of before the tribunal, the judges or magistrates rose, and the crowd immediately dispersed. I, too, shouldered my knapsack and departed on my way through the town. Shortly after leaving Pont l'Evêque it became showery, and then began to rain. I took refuge under a railway bridge for a time. A countryman who passes observes that this is not good weather for travelling, as indeed it is not. This casual remark sets me thinking as to what strange beings we Londoners are at this time of the year. We leave our luxurious and comfortable houses, lodgings, chambers, or rooms, as if the plague had set in, and leave home to encounter all kinds of annoyances and inconveniences. We crowd together in small lodgings at the sea-side, or jostle against one another at continental hotels. And last, though not least, here I am a solitary pedestrian, walking in the rain! Perhaps the true solution is that man, even in his most refined state, retains somewhat of the nature of the savage. He wishes for awhile to leave his own circle, to dismiss for a time the fetters, golden though they may be, of civilization, and to roam about with freedom and untrammelled by his daily cares and anxieties. And that the means of luxurious travel placed at the command of the wealthy do not adequately satisfy this natural craving is, I think, obvious from the circumstance that ordinary travellers always seem to dwell on the primitive mode of walking as the most enjoyable. Though unwilling to encounter the fatigue, discomfort, and occasional danger incurred by the pedestrian, they feel mentally, " Would that my mode of travel were like his!" And strange as it may seem, I have observed well-dressed, delicately-nurtured, and luxuriously-living ladies express and apparently feel great interest in pedestrianism. "How nice!" "I should so like to walk!"

Of course they would break down on the first day, and have to be escorted to a carriage. But still the sentiment seems nevertheless to prevail. This makes me hope that I may have many ladies among my readers, for they at least, while reclining on the sofa, or sitting out on the lawn, may follow in my footsteps without fatigue or discomfort.

Presently I leave the railway arch, but have not gone far before I have to encounter the worst storm of rain it is my lot to meet with during my travels in Normandy. I make for an outhouse, but only to find it barred with a padlock. The rain fell in torrents, and there I stood under the eaves of this outhouse in a hopelessly unprotected state, for the rain came through a strong new umbrella as if it had been a sieve. I never encountered such a steady downpour in England. There were some cottages not far off, but no sign of life about them; and to leave my refuge, imperfect as it was, for the chance of admittance there, would have made matters worse. Fortunately the storm was short-lived. Soon the sun began to appear through the dark clouds, and the rain to mitigate, and I proceeded on my way. I could not help now dwelling on the advantages of walking alone; for I must confess to feeling a little dull sometimes at the commencement of a pedestrian journey. I am sure my friend would thus early begin to talk of the danger of rheumatism and other ills, and be in favour of at once hiring a small covered carriage, and enforce his advice with ejaculatory observations as to the climate of the country such as I could not venture to print here. As it is, the genial sunshine and refreshing feel of the air make me soon forget the drenching I have received.

The country between Pont l'Evêque and Beuzeville is rather tame and uninviting, but not unpleasant walking. I have again omitted to note down the distance, but I think it must be about fourteen kilomètres (or eight miles). I did not reach Beuzeville until late in the evening, when it was quite dark. I found the two best inns in the place full, apparently on account of the next day, Sunday, being market day. So I went on further in the town to a small inn, where I obtained admittance, and was the only guest. The house was in a state of great disorder, it being washing-up night. From the immethodical nature of the arrangements I infer, what I believe to be the case, that my host is a widower. He has a daughter —a pretty girl—and a son, and, like some establishments I have seen at home, he is encumbered with too many servants. There are two or three about the house, which is a very small one, consequently nothing is well done or ready. A maid shows me to a bedroom which is in disorder. On coming downstairs, a pail of water is in the way, and in the dark I nearly step into it, and run the danger of falling head over heels into the kitchen. Two or three things are slowly got ready for my dinner; one of them part of a pig's head, so dry and antique-looking, that, had I seen it in a museum, labelled as portion of a wild boar killed by William the Conqueror in the New Forest, I should have considered the statement credible enough. My host, observing that I do not attack this *pièce de résistance*, comes up and cuts off parts of it, to show that it possesses some eatable qualities; and to please him rather than myself I use the knife, and find two or three slices more savoury than I could have expected from appearances. The only member of the household who seems actively engaged with a practical purpose is my host himself, who is concentrating his attention on a huge joint, or rather portion, of meat, which is roasting on a large turnspit before the fire, and which he is keeping in motion. Presently the cleaning and scrubbing are all over, and my host's pretty daughter sits down at this the last moment, to mend her cap ready for the morrow, Sunday.

However, though I criticise the arrangements, I am well pleased with my reception here. This being the first country inn I have stopped at in Normandy, I notice things more. Though I arrive late in the evening, and on a Saturday, when there is a general process of cleaning going on, and I am the only guest to be provided for, neither my host, nor his son and daughter, nor the servants, consider me at all in the way, but one and all are eager to administer to my comfort and wants. The disorder around is evidently only considered annoying because it may annoy me. Altogether, these my first experiences at a Norman country inn are favourable to my further progress through the country.

CHAPTER III.

An old custom—A clean cap—Department of Eure—Villages of St. Maclon, Tontainville, and St. Germain—About the roads—Distance between Beuzeville and Pont Audemer—No English there—Description of the town—Banks of the Rille—Good fishing—Hôtel Pont d'Etain—Provincial brogue—Nature of Norman towns—Epaignes, Cormeilles, and Hermival—A short cut—Distance between Pont Audemer and Lisieux—Re-enter Calvados—Lisieux—Old streets — Cathedral — Church of St. Jacques—Gardens—Corbon—A halt—Distance between Lisieux and Caen—Reflections on the Conquest—Roadside inns—A spectral dog—A humble wish—Suburbs of Caen—The midnight hour—Enter the streets of Caen—Solitude of a great city—Search for the Hôtel d'Angleterre—A friendly guide—A modest wish, though not realized—To the rescue.

Sunday, Sept. 6th. — At half-past five o'clock this morning some gendarmes were beating drums all through the town; but whether for military purposes, or in pursuance of an old custom, to wake the inhabitants, I could not discover. While at breakfast a townswoman entered the inn, and my host directed attention to her cap, which rose in a pyramidal form about half a yard above her head. It was beautifully clean and white, and the woman was pleased at the stranger's attention being directed to her cap, which was no doubt her Sunday best.

After breakfast I started for Pont Audemer. The country is pleasing, but without anything particularly interesting. Shortly before reaching Beuzeville I passed out of the department of Calvados into that of Eure, where I am now walking. On the way to Pont Audemer I pass through the villages of St. Maclon, Tontainville, and St. Germain. From Honfleur to Trouville the road is one of grand communication, that from Trouville to Pont l'Evêque and Beuzeville departmental. To-day, as far as the village of St. Maclon, the road is departmental, but there you fall into the imperial road from Honfleur, and proceed along that to Pont Audemer. I have again omitted to note down the distance between Beuzeville and Pont Audemer, but think it must be about sixteen kilomètres (or ten miles). I hurried a good deal, in order to be in time for the English church service, which, according to "Murray's

Handbook," is performed here on Sundays at No. 45, Rue de Bernay. However, though I looked about the town a good deal, I could neither find the street nor the service. Still, I made no inquiries on the subject, and therefore am not in a position to contradict the statement. But it is improbable. Pont Audemer lies altogether out of the track of ordinary tourists. I only observed one apparently English person, a gentleman going or returning from fishing. I was induced to visit this place through Mr. Musgrave's mention of it in his "Ramble in Normandy," and if my own pilgrimage there should induce any of my readers to do the same, I don't think they will be disappointed. Pont Audemer is a regular old Norman town, and presents a quaint appearance. I put up at the Hôtel Pont d'Etain. In the afternoon I walked along the banks of the Rille. The views from here are most beautiful; indeed, this walk is the principal attraction of the place. There are seats here and there. The river Rille runs along outside the town, and consequently this promenade is more rural, and less frequented by the townspeople, than it would otherwise be. I believe there is good fishing to be had at, or rather in the neighbourhood of, Pont Audemer. I saw several men and boys fishing on the banks of the Rille, but I did not perceive them catch anything.

At the Hôtel Pont d'Etain my host and hostess were sadly put-to to find any guests to make up a *table d'hôte* dinner. The bell rang long and loud, but after the lapse of half an hour no one presented himself. I heard the waiter observe to his mistress that he did not know how the dinner would be made up, as there was only "that gentleman," meaning myself. At length, two nondescript men from somewhere in the town—perhaps from among the by-ways of mine host's acquaintance—appeared, and we five sat down to a really good dinner, making it a pity there were not more to appreciate the Sunday fare. After dinner I strolled about the town, and took coffee at a café. The townspeople to-day, particularly the women, are idle with their tongues, or rather busy. I never heard anywhere else in Normandy such guttural, unpleasant sounds. When the voice was raised, and the talk became animated, the noise was something terrific. Here provincial French has evidently reached its climax, and reigns supreme, undisturbed by any of the genial influences of Parisian society.

Monday, Sept. 7th.—Before I proceed on my journey to-day, I may mention that in Normandy there are three descriptions of towns: the principal is the chief place of the department, very much equivalent to our cathedral towns; the next is the chief place of the arrondissement, a division of territory, the exact limits of which I must confess I do not know, except that there are several arrondissements in each department; the third and last kind of town is the chief place of the canton, a still more limited division of country than the arrondissement. The villages are communes, and beyond those there are, of course, hamlets, which, however, I presume, are attached to some neighbouring commune. To give instances of these towns, Havre, Pont l'Evêque, and Pont Audemer, are chief places of arrondissements; Honfleur and Beuzeville are chief places of cantons; while Trouville, though a flourishing little town, remains merely a commune. Nothing, however, so much as this fact serves to show the rapidity with which a sea-side resort will rise into popularity and importance. A few years since, doubtless, Trouville was in reality a village, and nothing more.

I left Pont Audemer early this morning for Lisieux. It was showery, though a pleasant walk, and through a fine country. I pass along a departmental road, and through the village of Epaignes, the canton town of Cormeilles, and the village of Hermival. There appears to be a shorter road of grand communication, by one kilomètre (or half a mile), coming into the main road at the village of La Chapelle. Those, therefore, who prefer on all occasions to consult the niceties of short-cuts should seek this road, which seems to branch off at the village of St. Germain, a little way out of the town of Pont Audemer, on the road to Beuzeville. Moreover, I find these roads of grand communication much pleasanter to walk upon. They are softer to the feet, through not becoming hardened by much traffic. The distance between Pont Audemer and Lisieux is thirty-six kilomètres (or twenty-two miles). A little beyond Cormeilles I passed out of the department of Eure, and re-entered that of Calvados.

On reaching Lisieux, which is the chief place of an arrondissement, I put up at the Hôtel de Commerce, an inn not mentioned in "Murray's Handbook," but recommended by Musgrave in his " Ramble in Normandy." I found the inn very clean, comfortable, and moderate. The *table d'hôte* dinner was at six o'clock. With the exception of myself, all who sat down were Frenchmen.

Tuesday, Sept. 8th.—This morning I walked about the town of Lisieux, to see the place. It looks curiously old, and contains many streets with wooden houses and strange signs. In the Rue du Fauvres, in particular, there is an old wooden house very singular in appearance. The cathedral—or what was formerly such—is a fine building, both as to the exterior and interior, but still very plain and devoid of ornament. The Lady Chapel is particularly simple. The Church of St. Jacques is worth inspecting for its painted windows, Lady Chapel, and otherwise. At the back of the bishop's palace there are some beautiful gardens, with an avenue of trees, with seats here and there, beds of flowers, and in the centre a pool of water, with two or three ducks. There is a statue at the extremity of the gardens, but to whom I could not discover. The gardens are kept in prime order, and must serve as a fine promenade for the inhabitants of Lisieux.

Having had some breakfast at a café, I returned to the Hôtel de Commerce, but only to leave immediately, *en route* for Caen. It was twelve o'clock before I started, much too late, as it turned out, to enable me in comfort to reach my forced destination. I walk along the imperial road, and through the villages of Bousquetterie, La Boissiére, and Grévecœur, to Corbon. Here there is a small inn, where I stop to halt and rest, and have some luncheon of biscuits and pear cider. I think a bed might be obtained here, as it is something above a roadside inn, and the pedestrian who does not start early from Lisieux, or feel equal to the fatigue of a thirty miles' walk, should rest at this place for the night.

After leaving Corbon, I passed through the villages of Bieville, Le Bras d'Or, Le Lion d'Or, Croissanville, and several other villages. The distance between Lisieux and Caen is forty-eight kilomètres (or twenty-nine miles). The country is flat and barren-looking, at least as regards scenery. There is no town of any kind, but only a succession of very small villages and hamlets. Here and there a gentleman's carriage passed me. The whole country side is but sparsely populated. Nowhere else in Normandy was I more impressed with the greatness of the scheme of conquest devised and successfully carried out by William the Conqueror, than during the thirty miles' walk between Lisieux and Caen. Here, even in the neighbourhood of the capital of the country, there are few inhabitants scattered about this long distance eight hundred years after the event. I can imagine how the rival barons must have scoffed at the idea of the enterprise proposed for their consideration by William, Duke of Normandy. Where the ships, where the troops for so great an undertaking? And then one sees at the head of the council board the stern duke, listening with calmness and patience to the numerous objections raised to the project, for he must conciliate them all—yes, even the least—for he can afford to spare none. All the barons of this thinly-populated country, and their armed retainers, must be gathered together, and made to bend to one strong will and far-seeing mind, or England cannot be conquered. And then, not at any single gathering of barons, but at many meetings, the great and persevering Duke of Normandy removes all the objections to his project, and argues away the difficulties, and the preparations are commenced which are destined to bring about one of the most important conquests which has ever been made in the world's history.

It was nightfall before I had walked much more than half-way to Caen. This was most provoking, as with proper management and by leaving Lisieux early I might easily have accomplished the day's journey in reasonable time. But I proposed to myself a short stage only to-day, relying as a matter of course on meeting with an inn somewhere midway. However, I inquired at several village and road-side inns this evening, and could not obtain a bed anywhere. Indeed, at most of these country inns they do not appear to make up any beds, or profess to provide sleeping accommodation of any description. "*Ne couche pas ici*" is the friendly greeting which at nightfall reaches the ear of the weary traveller. I am reminded of Don Quixote's first day's journey from home, in Spain, where it seems the same inconvenient if not inhospitable custom prevails. The Don, on reaching his inn, was courteously received by the landlord, and in reply to the question as to what could be had, answered, " Everything except a bed." So here to-night I am in the same predicament. At these wayside inns I observe people eating, drinking, and smoking, and carousing to their hearts' content, but they must find sleeping quarters elsewhere. I found one exception, indeed, if such it could be called. I entered a wayside inn. There were people, including two or three young women, sitting round a table drinking cider, and apparently more than enough. The master of the house somewhat unsteadily handed me a rickety chair, on which I sat down, but no one appearing to move, I asked to see the bedroom I was told I could have. An elderly woman, I presume the mistress, then escorted me upstairs and showed me a large room with three or four beds in it. I asked if I could occupy the room alone. The reply was, No, I could have one of the beds. Had the people about the house been more sober and respectable-looking, tired as I was, I should have accepted this accommodation; but under the existing circumstances I declined it, and made my way down the dark staircase and into the road, as best I could without a light, for the mistress seemed offended at my notion of having a bedroom to myself.

Shortly afterwards, to the left of the highroad, I see a number of lights indicative of a small town; but I perceive no road in that direction, and so am compelled to trudge on. I was dreadfully fatigued, for apart from the circumstance that I had been walking for several hours about Lisieux before I started, I had not been long enough on my travels to be in proper condition for such a journey. Indeed, on one occasion in the faint light—for there was no moon at all full—I saw a large dog cross the road just before me; but immediately perceived it must be a spectral one, the result of excessive fatigue. No doubt, as the body weakens, the powers of correct perception, whether of the eye or mind, diminish and gradually fade away. Therefore, dear reader, if you have any friend on whose judgment or sagacity you would wish to rely, seek it while his body is strong and mind sound. Never mind the hilarious laugh of lusty health, or the ill-timed wit with which the good advice may be interspersed. You may safely rely upon it now. But if you wait until the dread hand of some mortal disease has seized your friend, then, if even you have the good fortune to obtain access to his sick-room, you will find your friend's mind wandering, his perreptions faint, no smile, no wit; but at the same time, no sagacity, no judgment, no sound sense; and before you have been many minutes by the bed-side you will be requested to remove that black man who is standing there, appearing, alas! plainly enough before the eye, to which disease has given the strange power of a deceptive imagination.

I walk on, and sit down to rest awhile on a heap of stones, when sharp and clear through the night air come the tones of the church clocks of Caen. They are striking eleven o'clock, and prove welcome enough, as showing that the city is not far off; but sound is proverbially deceptive, and so it proves in the present instance. I am still some distance from any semblance of the suburbs of Caen, and now I begin to regret I had not stopped for refreshment at one of the wayside inns, for I feel a burning thirst; and then I amuse myself by considering that if a kind fairy were suddenly to present herself, and offer me anything I liked to drink, what I should prefer. Would it be champagne, claret, port, sherry, beer, spirits, soda-water, lemonade? No, none of these, but the drink of the country, a good draught of cider! But surely this moderate wish may be satisfied at the Hôtel d'Angleterre, whither I am bound, and without the aid of any fairy.

At length I reach a lamp-post, with the light still burning, and indicating that I am now in the suburbs of Caen. The road proceeds down a steep hill. I don't know how long it would seem to the visitor who comes to Caen in the ordinary way, and having exhausted the lions of the place saunters up this hill and through the suburbs, in order to catch a glimpse of the country beyond; but to myself, prostrated by fatigue, it appeared on this night to be a long and weary tramp. When I entered the city the clocks were striking twelve o'clock, and the hour of midnight having arrived, all the street and other lamps were put out; and there being no moon, the whole place became devoted to darkness. I began to fear I should have to spend the night out wandering about the streets, perhaps passing and repassing many an inn, for I could not distinguish the houses. However, presently I hear in the distance the welcome sound of the step of a gendarme going his beat; so I make up to him, and ask the way to the Hôtel d'Angleterre. He civilly gives me the direction, which I follow out for a time, but soon become lost amid the mazes of a strange city enveloped in darkness. No living soul is about anywhere; all is still. There is something almost awe-striking about the silence and solitude of a great city; the work, and turmoil, and pleasure of the day are over, and for a few hours at least a certain kind of equality prevails among all classes. The rich, indeed, are reposing on beds of down, and the poor with only a single blanket around them; but kind nature's sweet refresher sleep has come alike to all, giving fresh energy and strength to renew the daily struggle for bread, or the daily round of amusement and relaxation.

While absorbed in these thoughts, and doubtful what to do or whither to turn my footsteps, a young gentleman passes me. I am in luck's way now. I ask him which is the Hôtel d'Angleterre. He answers politely that he will show me it, as he is going through the street on his way home. This is most assuring, and places me at ease. We walk on, and down the Rue St. Jean, and reach the hotel; but the lamp there is extinguished, and all in darkness. My kind friend says he will ring the bell, but this is much easier said than done. He feels and fumbles about for a long time in vain. I ask him whether there is really any bell at all there. "Oh, yes, a very large one." And sure enough the handle, as I observed next day, was large and conspicuous, so much so as to raise a retrospective feeling of wonder at our present difficulty. Presently I tried to find the handle of the bell, but with no better success. The position we were in was certainly ridiculous, and my young friend was highly amused at our difficulties, as he observed he passed the hotel every day, and knew it very well; but, as Lord Lytton states in one of his valuable essays, we do not note down and observe things which are daily before us; and he remarks of himself, that he could better describe the banks of the Nile than those of the stream running through the grounds of the house where he was born, and where he hopes to die. It has been truly said that "necessity is the mother of invention." A sudden thought strikes me that to this huge door before which we are standing there must be a knocker. I ask my friend. He thinks so too. Accordingly I commence feeling over the centre of the door, and soon find a large knocker, which I at once rap loud enough to awake the seven sleepers. A porter opens the door at once—so quickly, indeed, that I am surprised he did not hear our voices outside. I thank my young friend, and wish him good night. I enter the Hôtel d'Angleterre, and ask the porter to give me a glass of cider. He has none. Something to eat. Nor that either. A glass of water. That I shall find in my room. There was a kind of cruelty about the refusal of the cider, though arising from inability, of which, of course, the porter was unaware. But I am afraid my wish is but a counterpart of what often occurs in the more important affairs of life. You may as well wish for the claret or champagne as for the plebeian cider. If you are a soldier, you may as well wish for the baton of the field-marshal as the command of a regiment; if a sailor, to be admiral of the red, white, or blue—whichever is highest, for at this moment I forget—as to be post-captain; if a clergyman, for the mitre of the bishop instead of the modest living; if a lawyer, you may as well aspire to the woolsack as seek to obtain any subordinate office, for in your case the highest position of all may prove as unattainable as the humble shelf upon which you may have set your heart.

However, the porter at the Hôtel d'Angleterre was an honest fellow enough, prepared to do his duty, and nothing more. Indeed, he informed me that all the things were locked up, and that he could only show me to a bedroom, which he did accordingly, and a good one too; and then departed, making his way with difficulty down the dark stairs. I drank some water to quench the burning thirst, and soon sought that sleep which so often proves welcome, not only to the weary, but also to the hungry and thirsty, and it quickly came to my rescue.

CHAPTER IV.

A swarm of flies—Caen—Church of St. Pierre—St. Etienne or Abbaye aux Hommes—Grave of the Conqueror—Reflections thereon—St. Etienne le Vieux—Abbaye aux Dames or La Sainte Trinité—Church of St. Jean—St. Savern— Public school of the Lycée—Present appearance of Caen— Quays—Avenues of trees—Table d'hôte at Hôtel d'Angleterre—Set out for Bayeux—Village of Maladrerie—Quarries of stone—An old ruin—A lift—Bretteville—Bayeux— Hôtel du Luxembourg—The tapestry—Cathedral—A punctual host—Chapelle de Séminaire—Return to Caen—Church at Norrey—Caen again—Hôtel de Victoire—Place Royale— Hôtel de Ville—An uncivil porter—Philosophy from a little child—Compulsory courtesy—A nondescript party—A welcome escape—A sumptuous repast—A hotel for the lover of good cheer.

Wednesday, Sept. 9th.—While at breakfast this morning I am attacked and surrounded by a regular swarm of flies, such as I have not hitherto met with. I am much annoyed by their personal attentions to myself, since, after my long walk yesterday and unchanged dress, it may result from uncleanliness; but presently, to my great relief, there comes and sits down near me an elderly gentleman, extremely prim, neat, and well-dressed, evidently a luxurious first-class traveller, whereupon the flies, *en masse*, immediately leave me, and settle round and about the new comer: thus setting my mind at rest on this small matter. Some of them, indeed, afterwards return, but not in the same number.

I remained to-day at Caen, and after breakfast sallied forth to see the lions of the place, and was thus engaged until dinner-time. The most celebrated object in church architecture at Caen is the church of St. Pierre. It is, however, the spire, more than any other part of the building, which has attracted so much attention. This is certainly very striking. It rises to a great height, and tapers towards the point so gradually and imperceptibly as to present to the eye of the lay beholder a spire of beautiful form and dimensions. I can well imagine an architect being struck with admiration at the skill displayed in the construction of the tower and spire, the difficulties of which he would be so well able to appreciate and recognize. The spire of St. Pierre is a conspicuous object, not only iu Caen itself, but from the surrounding country, and is, no doubt, a subject of just pride to the inhabitants. The interior of the church of St. Pierre, however, is somewhat plain in appearance, giving the idea that the chief care had been bestowed on the tower. But the small chapels around the high altar are very elegantly adorned with roofs finely worked.

The most interesting of the churches at Caen to visit is that of St. Etienne, or Abbaye aux Hommes. Here is the burying-place of William the Conqueror. The present church occupies the site of the old building. It is very plain indeed, both outside and inside, but nevertheless from the size assumes a grand appearance. The sacristy formed a chapel of the original building, and is I believe the only part of the structure now remaining. There is here an ancient picture of William the Conqueror. Near the high altar is a plain stone of white marble, enclosed by a border of coloured marble, altogether about the size of an ordinary gravestone. It contains the inscription, " Hic sepultus est," etc., and so well written, that time, which plays so much havoc with ordinary inscriptions, is not likely to obliterate it. The remains of the Conqueror were removed, though I forget when, or the circumstances, and no longer remain deposited here, their first resting-place. According to Mr. Musgrave, the Latin commencement signifies " Here *was* buried." Whether or not these Latin words are capable of so refined a construction, I must leave my classical readers to determine. All I can say is, that if so, the idea is a fine one.

As I stand on the spot which *was* the grave of William the Conqueror, I seem in fancy to be carried back eight hundred years. The present modern church vanishes, and an old primitive structure takes its place. Before and around me are priests in golden vestments, choristers in rude garments of spotless white, knights in armour, and among them one more distinguished-looking and sorrowful than the rest, Henry, the King's son. Then there is gathered together a motley assemblage of all ranks and classes, and both sexes, the young, the feeble, and the old. In the midst of all, on rough trestles, is placed the clumsily constructed coffin containing the remains of William the Conqueror. The solemn service for the dead is about to begin, when a common fellow from among the assembled crowd rushes forward and claims the ground where the grave has been dug, and forbids the ceremony to proceed. A claim so astounding and inopportune is at once resisted, but it stands nevertheless confirmed by a hundred voices. Then I see a knight slowly and grimly counting out the large pieces of silver money, the price of the ground, and contemptuously throwing them towards the seller. Now, at length, the service proceeds, but only to be again arrested, and this time by a circumstance truly appalling. The grave is too small, and in thrusting down the coffin, it bursts, and the body breaks out. The effluvium is sickening. The priests hurry through their office, and the varied crowd disperse as quickly as possible, driven by nausea from the deadly presence of the mighty chieftain whom they would have considered a high honour to be near when alive. I think no one can have read of these sad rites of sepulture without feelings of pity, and regret that a life so memorable should have been closed with a burial under circumstances so humiliating to human grandeur. But presently my thoughts seem to rise from the grave beneath me, and assume a less earthly aspect. I reflect on the noble spirit which once tenanted that loathsome corpse; how, during all the centuries which have followed, it has seemed to live, and act, and pervade the history of my country; and how, on the foundation-stone which he laid, a splendid constitutional building has been raised, the admiration and wonder of the world. And then I dwell on the fact of the countless thousands who have visited this spot as a shrine hallowed by glorious associations, and have recognized in the duke, the king, the man who was buried here, the founder of the greatness and power of Britain.

Not far from St. Etienne is an old church called St. Etienne le Vieux. It has, however, not been used for divine worship for twenty-one years, and is now turned into a carpenter's shop and a depository of wood. The church, however, is very curious, and worth inspecting, though it cannot be seen without some unpleasantness, unless the ownership of the place has changed hands; for no sooner had I entered the building than a man came up and told me it was closed to the public—a fact of course obvious enough, though, as no possible harm could be done by walking about, I continued to do so. The fellow, however, followed me about in an impertinent manner; and when I reached the yard to see the back of the building, he threatened to unchain a large dog there, and to send him at me. However, I took no notice of this conduct beyond, perhaps, continuing in the building longer than I should otherwise have done. And I should recommend the reader who may be similarly treated to pursue a like course towards any such insolent intruder on his pleasure. I believe this building belongs to the municipality, and if so, this fellow no doubt is armed with that little brief authority, the nature and effects of which have been so eloquently described by Shakspeare, though in a passage too well known to be quoted here. I saw another curious old church at Caen which is used as a storehouse.

At the other end of Caen there is the church of Abbaye aux Dames, or La Sainte Trinité, which I visited. It is a stately edifice, but the interior of which I could not see, as it was closed for repairs. I also visited the church of St. Jean, in the street of that name, where, however, there is nothing particular; and the church of St. Savern, which is remarkably plain inside, but with a fine exterior. The Lady Chapel, however, is singular, and worth inspecting.

I visited the public school of the Lycée Impériale, which is close near the church of St. Etienne. It is a place extremely interesting to look over. I applied at the *concierge*, and a young woman appeared to attend me through the building. She was very plain, but her modesty of manner, civility, and intelligence much impressed me. Finding that I was curious, she showed and explained everything. The *salle à manger* is a large and commodious room. There are three meals a-day. The bed-rooms are arranged in long corridors, each separate from the others, and complete in itself. The rooms face large windows with the wood-work pierced, so the ventilation must be very good. The most is also made of the space. There is a better bed-room for each of the masters. A large room, with about half-a-dozen beds in a row, is set apart for small boys, from two or three to seven years of age, with a bedroom overlooking it for the *maîtresse* who attends them. The infirmary is fitted up with a better class of rooms—some separate as the rest, and others with two or three beds in the same room. Every comfort is here, such as arm-chairs, so that the young patient is altogether much better accommodated than when well. Including out-boarders, the scholars are about a thousand. In the entrance-chamber are ranged round the room tablets containing a statement of the names of the boys who have obtained prizes, and their position in the school, extending over a period of upwards of thirty years. This is a very convenient practice, as it enables any employer of a youth to ascertain readily and without doubt his scholastic acquirements.

Caen, though so full of historic associations, does not present by any means an antiquated appearance. There are some curious old houses in the Rue St. Pierre, which probably formed part of the old city, which *may* have replaced that which existed at the time of the Conquest. I walked on the quays, which form spacious and quiet promenades. Here there were some English children playing about. In the distance are avenues of trees. It was now time to return to the *table d'hôte* dinner at the Hôtel d'Angleterre. There were assembled some English people, the first I had met since leaving Trouville; indeed, I think the majority of those present were of my own country, and the inn, therefore, well deserves its name.

Thursday, Sept. 10th.—This morning I set out on a walk to Bayeux, twenty-seven kilomètres (or seventeen miles) from Caen. Shortly after leaving Caen, I pass through the village of La Maladrerie. Near here are the celebrated quarries of Caen stone. I observe the wheels above the shafts. I believe anybody who so pleases may, by applying to the manager in charge, descend these quarries, a visit to which would no doubt prove very interesting. About two miles from Caen, I walked across a field to observe an old ruin in the distance, near a farmhouse, which, however, seemed scarcely worthy of a closer inspection. Soon afterwards I was overtaken by a young man in a cabriolet, or *voiture*, who gave me a lift for about ten miles, until he turned off from the main road, about five kilomètres (or three miles) from Bayeux. I found my friend an agreeable companion. We pass through Bretteville and other villages, at one of which we stop to bait the horse. My friend, on stopping, receives a most genial welcome at the wayside inn, so I presume he is a commercial traveller, well known along this road.

On entering Bayeux, a woman asks me the way to a particular street, which, to me, arriving here for the first time in my life, sounds oddly enough. I reply that I am a stranger, and she politely apologizes for the mistake. I put up at the Hôtel du Luxembourg. This is a quiet and comfortable inn, with a pretty garden attached, which affords a pleasing prospect from my bed-room window, though I did not walk about there. Bayeux consists of two main streets—the one by which you enter being old, and characteristic of Norman towns; the other quite a modern street.

I went to the public library and had a leisurely inspection of the celebrated tapestry, and with the advantage of being alone, as it was not a public day. I found the tapestry about as I expected, but more quaint and rough, and the figures not so well formed as I anticipated, but altogether very curious and interesting. If not so old as the Conquest, and if they do not owe their origin to the Queen Matilda, the tapestry, beyond all doubt, must be very ancient. The figures consist of a series of descriptions of the preparations and events connected with the Conquest: such as the departure of the ships; the landing of the troops; and, to an Englishman, most striking and affecting of all, Harold being killed on the field of battle at Hastings by a Norman knight, and in the act of rising to defend himself. Each tableau has a Latin inscription, descriptive of the scene illustrated. That about Harold is simple, touching, and dignified, and worthy of the wife of the Conqueror. His title is not disputed here! No vain-glorious boast is recorded at the fall of one against whom such mighty preparations were made. The event of the soldier's death is merely stated as a fact, which could not indeed have been omitted without rendering incomplete the whole history of the Conquest. It is simply this: "Hic rex interfectus est." The tapestry, I believe, was formerly unrolled to the view of the visitors, now, however, it is arranged permanently on screens round the room, and you can take your own time in looking at the different tableaux, which is much more convenient.

Afterwards I visited the cathedral at Bayeux.

This strikes me as by far the most magnificent church I have yet seen in Normandy. Both the exterior and interior are in the extreme grand and sublime, and calculated to arrest and fix the attention of the most callous stranger. However, so singularly insensible does the mind become to the daily sight of the sublime and beautiful, that the inhabitants of Bayeux seem unconscious of anything striking or remarkable about the stately edifice, under the shadow of which they have been born and carry on their occupations; for while I was standing gazing at the stupendous pile of buildings before me, a small knot of persons assembled and began discussing what the stranger could be looking at. At length one of them, more sagacious than the rest, arrived at a decision, which he gravely propounded to the others. "He is looking at the cathedral." The answer seemed to give complete satisfaction, for almost immediately the small crowd dispersed, and I was left alone still looking upward.

Then I entered the interior of the cathedral, and saw the sacristy and the crypt, which latter contains on the pillars some curious figures, but many of them quite defaced. Near the altar, just beneath the steps, and also outside the rails of the choir, are simple memorials on the stone to the memory of those who have been bishops of Bayeux from the thirteenth century until recently; but apparently in no regular order or succession, so some of them must be buried in other parts of the edifice, or perhaps requested that no memorial should record their place of sepulture. These memorials contain a simple statement of the name and time of death of the deceased bishop, except in one instance, where the age (eighty) is stated.

It was now time to return to the Hôtel du Luxembourg to dinner. My host proved quite a disciplinarian, and in this remote town set an example which is worthy to be followed in more frequented places. Precisely as the bell rang for the *table d'hôte* he entered the *salle à manger*, and seated himself at the head of the table, though I was the only guest present. The dinner was immediately served, and the soup had been removed to a side table before any other guest appeared. Then they came in one by one, most, if not all of them, I think, arriving from the town and not staying in the house. One of them rallied my host for not waiting for the company, which, when assembled, amounted to a goodly number, about twelve; but he replied quietly that he never waited for any one, and the answer seemed to raise him in the estimation of his guests. I may observe, also, that ceremony alone did not prevail at this table. My host was not only punctual, but also hospitable. The dinner was good, substantial, and well served.

In the evening I visited the Chapelle de Séminaire, of the date 1206. It is very plain and simple, but some painted windows add a little to the ornament of the chapel. Two or three of the windows have white glass, so probably this was the early condition of all of them. I could not find the recess behind the altar, which seems formerly to have existed, so perhaps it has been removed. It was twilight while I was standing in this old primitive-looking chapel, and there was something sombre about the scene. Presently my reverie was broken by the arrival of a priest, who seemed surprised at my presence. He lit up the chapel, then two or three women appeared, I presume for the confessional, and I departed.

Friday, Sept. 11*th.*—I left Bayeux this

morning on my way back to Caen, distant, I may repeat, twenty-seven kilomètres (or seventeen miles). I started early, and took breakfast at Bretteville. I then left the high-road—which, by the way, between Caen and Bayeux, is imperial—and proceeded along a road of grand communication to visit the church at Norrey, which is considered a miniature cathedral. I only saw the outside of the building, the church being closed, and I did not feel disposed to seek out the person who held possession of the key, which, however, I afterwards regretted. I should recommend the reader to give himself this trouble. The exterior of the church looks fine and symmetrical, and I can well imagine that the interior would bear out the description it has received.

On reaching Caen I put up at the Hôtel de Victoire, which I was desirous to try, as it is celebrated for its *cuisine*. I was shown to a good room, and having settled down here, I then went to the Place Royale, as I wished to see the collection of paintings in the Hôtel de Ville. It was not, however, one of the days when the place is open, and on my requesting of the porter leave to see the pictures, as I was a stranger, and should be quitting Caen tomorrow, he suddenly became very insolent, and refused my request point blank. As his conduct differed so much from that of the French generally in their manner to strangers, I apprehend he may have been visiting on me ill-usage he had received from others of my countrymen, who probably had taken a private view without giving him a gratuity, or one adequate to his ideas of sufficiency on such an occasion.

This fellow's insolence quite disturbed me, and sitting down on a seat in the square, I fell into a brown study. A little child, a girl who could just walk, came up and began playing at my knee, and, almost unconsciously to myself, took out of my hand a centime I had been mechanically fumbling. Presently she returned, bringing from her mother and friends, who were sitting on an adjoining seat, a plaster cast of the Virgin Mary, which she put into my hand. I returned it to the child and she to me, when I began to perceive her meaning, that in return for the centime I was to receive the only thing she had to give in exchange, the cast of the Virgin. I placed the image again in the child's hand, but she watching the opportunity, put it suddenly down on my knee, and toddled off. After awhile, the mother came and took the image away, apologizing for the child's interruption. I allude thus in detail to this small incident, because it shows in a remarkable manner that which philosophers are ever in search of, how ideas of things first enter our infant minds. No doubt this child, while yet in arms, had observed its mother enter a shop, put down a coin, and receive something in exchange. Therefore when the child took my centime, she considered it just and proper that I should have in exchange the only thing she had to offer, the image of the Virgin Mary. This idea would be one of sensation, to adopt the classification founded by Locke in his immortal " Essay on the Human Understanding;" the idea of value would be one of reflection, according to the same writer. Certainly on the present occasion I should have been a considerable gainer by the transaction, as the plaster cast could not well have cost less than half a franc.

But I rise from my seat and philosophy vanishes. There is a statue in the centre of the Place Royale, but to whom I could not discover, as it contains no inscription. On returning to the Hôtel de Victoire I was met by my hostess with the most profuse apologies; a large party of English had just arrived, who required rooms *en suite*, of which mine was one; she felt sure I would oblige my countrymen; in fact she had already removed my things to another room. There was no help for it but to bear this compulsory courtesy on my part in good humour, so I assented to all mine hostess had said on my behalf. At dinner I sat near the party I had obliged. They were rather nondescript. One of them was an old pleasant-looking gentleman, apparently married to the younger, plain, and imperious woman sitting by his side. Then there was a lady relative or friend who seemed rather overawed. The result of this apparently ill-assorted union was very successful in the shape of offspring, for there were two interesting-looking, well-behaved young girls on the other side of the table from me, who were ventilating their French very prettily with a lady sitting next them. I remained silent, not altogether liking my neighbours. The imperious woman wondered what travellers meant by calling the Norman women beautiful, as she had certainly not seen any such as yet. "No," thought I, "nor you ever will." Then, turning to the old gentleman, who had probably been sight-seeing all day, she observed to his manifest horror, that there remained the avenue of trees to be done after dinner. Now my turn came. "I wonder," she said, "where Monsieur Anglais can be sitting; we must find him out after dinner, and thank him for giving up his room; I suppose that must be he," pointing to a stout, elderly gentleman sitting at the other end of the table, and who certainly looked somewhat John Bull-like. Thanks to my beard and moustache giving a foreign appearance, I remained unsuspected, so I ate my dinner in silence. The repast was certainly sumptuous, consisting of, I am afraid to say how many courses, and among them, no doubt to tempt the English here, potatoes done in three or four different ways. The lover of good living should certainly come here. Moreover, the hotel is quiet, unpretending, and moderate in its charges. I may observe that it is situated in the Place St. Pierre.

CHAPTER V.

Wasps—Falaise—A holy calm, where to be found—Churches of St. Gervais and Ste. Trinité—An awkward predicament—A singular custom—Guibray—Castle of Falaise—Birthplace of William the Conqueror—Tradition of Arlotte—Tower of the castle—Exterior view—The Val d'Ante—Kissing among men—Statue to William the Conqueror—Hôtel de Normandie—Scenery of Calvados— A drunken landlord—Out of Calvados into Orne— Argentan—Écouché—Briouze—Flers — Tinchebray—Story of the battle—Re-enter Calvados—Vire—Church of Notre Dame—A coffin lying in state—Walks and castle—Hôtel St. Pierre—Fulfilment of a promise.

Saturday, Sept. 12th.—To-day I walked from Caen to Falaise, thirty-four kilomètres (or twenty-one miles), along the imperial road. I breakfasted at an *auberge*, a short distance on the way. About mid-day I stopped at another *auberge*, and had a half bottle of cider. I find numerous wasps about the inns during my travels, and yet I do not observe any nests near the roads, so I suppose they are in the woods far away. Here, at this *auberge*, I am amused by watching two vigorous wasps who have fallen into common peril in an empty cider bottle. One of them, by many steady, well-directed efforts, almost succeeds in escaping up the neck of the bottle, the other never gets more than half way. At length it makes towards its more successful friend in adversity, as if to obtain information how to proceed. I feel much inclined to release them both, as they have displayed so much pluck and cunning, but already I have been chased round the room two or three times, during this period of rest, by their comrades in the enjoyment of liberty, so I forbear. A sting probably would be the reward of my philanthropy.

All the way between Caen and Falaise there are only villages, and those very few and small. The scenery is rural but by no means striking. A wavy kind of hilly scenery, part of the route, is the most worthy of notice. On entering Falaise, you have a good view of the castle and of the church of St. Gervais. I took up my quarters at the Hôtel de Normandie. After dinner, I strolled into the church of St. Gervais. There is a certain holy calm pervading the churches in Roman Catholic countries, especially of an evening, which is very pleasing to the lonely traveller, affording a rest to the weary mind which cannot be found elsewhere. I hope such feelings are not inconsistent with the staunchest and most orthodox Protestantism. Constantly after the *table d'hôte* dinner during my wanderings through Normandy did I adjourn to one of the churches, and taking possession of a chair, remain there awhile, not for prayer, but for rest, quiet change, and meditation on things in general. It seemed strange, indeed, to enter a gorgeous cathedral, or magnificent church dedicated to God, and yet not be allowed to pray there; to remain within the sacred precincts, and yet to shrink from entertaining any religious feelings; there to be seated among worshippers of the same common Father, and yet not to join with them in praise and thanksgiving. But this is one of those strange and mysterious anomalies of the Christian faith, too deep and difficult to be entered on here.

Sunday, Sept. 13th.—In the morning I visited the churches of St. Gervais and Ste. Trinité. In both buildings the exterior of the church is the most striking. In St. Gervais there are some statues of saints on the pillars at the back of the choir. I remained in this church during a great part of the service, and had seated myself where, perhaps, I ought not to have been, among the worshippers. Presently a priest came by with a basket full of small bread-crusts, and offered it to each person. Some took one piece, and others two or three pieces. When he came to me, observing, I presume, a stranger, he handed the basket very graciously, but on my refusing to take any crust, he turned scowlingly away, probably divining the reason. Perhaps there would have been no harm in partaking of a single piece of bread in this way. I think I should do so another time. I was certainly sorry to wound the good priest's feelings. I presume that these crusts of bread had nothing to do with the communion, being thus brought out among the congregation generally. Certainly I was never placed in a similar predicament before in any Roman Catholic church. You are never called upon to take any active part *against* the services going on there. Perhaps this custom is peculiar to Falaise. But herein I may very likely display my ignorance of much travel. You, dear reader, may have seen it at Rome, Naples, Venice, and a hundred other places. Another custom prevails at the church of St. Gervais, which I at least have not seen elsewhere. Two young girls assisted in collecting the offertory. They were dressed in white, with white veils, and looked extremely pretty and romantic. When, therefore, I state that I resisted even this appeal to my feelings, no doubt the reader will consider my Protestantism above all suspicion.

After leaving the church of St. Gervais, I walked up to see the castle, but was informed by the custodian's daughter—a fine-looking young woman—that her father was away at mass, and would not be back to show me over it until two o'clock; so I spent the interval in paying a visit to the interesting suburb of Guibray, about two kilomètres (or a mile and a half) from Falaise, though adjoining the town, being, in fact, a continuation of it. Guibray is celebrated for its fair, said to have been established by William the Conqueror. I entered the church of Guibray. There are some old monuments on the stone near the high altar. There is nothing particular about the interior of the church, but the outward view is very picturesque. Near the church are some curious old houses, now shut up, being only used at the time of the fair. The whole locality just round the church of Guibray still wears a very ancient appearance, though the surrounding neighbourhood is quite modern, being, indeed, a flourishing suburb of Falaise.

I then returned to the castle, and had the good fortune to reach the place just at two o'clock. The custodian was on the watch for his customer, and we proceeded together to view the castle. It is a fine, well-preserved old ruin, and the thick walls still remain in good condition. I entered the chamber which is supposed by tradition to have been the place where William the Conqueror was born. It is a small, square, dark-looking room, enclosed by stout walls. There is an inscription at the further end, rudely written on a rough tablet of wood, placed there, I believe, by a Frenchman some years ago. I did not copy the inscription, but it is to the following effect:—" Reader, he who was born here, if measured by men living in more civilized times, would be considered a barbarian; but if the primitive age when he lived be taken into account, he must be reckoned a very great man." The inscription is in French. I was highly amused at the simple idea entertained by this benevolent Frenchman. The inscription and tablet are certainly worthy of the age described. But tradition has marked the birthplace of William the Conqueror in characters more enduring than those written on brass or marble; and should the time ever come when these ruins shall have crumbled to dust, and no vestige of them remain above the ground, visitors will still come here from the most distant parts of the earth, and ask to be shown the spot where stood the castle, in a chamber of which the great founder of the British monarchy was born.

Close adjoining the chamber, the birthplace of the Conqueror, are two windows in the massive walls, from which Robert Duke of Normandy, according to the tradition, first saw Arlotte, the tanner's beautiful daughter, washing in the stream in the valley below. Mr. Musgrave throws doubt on the credibility of the story, on the ground that *he* could not distinguish, from the height of these walls, anything clearly or distinctly in the valley below. There is, however, something about the bend of a young girl's neck, a play of the waist, a graceful turn of the arms, a plasticity of movement, if I may so speak, about the whole figure, which render her perceptible at a great distance. For instance, at this very moment I see from these walls a woman washing linen in a pool in the valley just beneath. Now I venture to affirm, from personal observation merely, that this woman, save the mark—remember I am treating of a historical fact, and therefore gallantry should be laid aside—is neither young nor beautiful; but elderly at least, if not old. Therefore, on this ground, I think that there is nothing incredible in the circumstances as related in history of the pretty traditionary story, which we have all been accustomed from early childhood to receive as true.

The tower of the castle at Falaise is more completely preserved than that of any other part of the fortress. I ascended it, and mounted on to a modern-constructed roof of lead. From here a most extensive view is obtained of the town of Falaise and the surrounding country, and of the opposite heights. Altogether the castle is a most interesting old ruin. Afterwards I walked a great part round it, thus obtaining a good exterior view. I was particularly struck with the massive structure of the walls, which seem to bid defiance to the assaults of time. At one spot I sat down on the grassy turf of the mound above. The sun was shining brightly, and all around was still and silent; the castle looked grand and romantic, and the scene would have been one of striking grandeur for the pen of the artist to depict.

I then descended into the Val d'Ante, the birthplace of Arlotte, the tanner's fair daughter, who, whether the tradition concerning her first meeting with her royal lover be true or not, has become inseparably connected with the early history of this country. The houses in the valley all bear a very modern aspect, but the stream still flows on, and tanneries are still there, as in the days of old, centuries ago. On leaving the valley, I could not help reflecting on the scenes connected with William the Conqueror again and again. Though not in proper order, I have now visited the spot where the great king was born, have seen the tapestry where his achievements are recorded, and stood on the grave where his body was buried, with intended pomp and splendour, indeed, but, in fact, amid a scene of shame and indignity.

Then I walked into the town, and out again at a gateway of the old fortifications, and by a path along the ravines to a suburb where there is a little church, and back through a dismantled gateway. The good people of Falaise are all dressed in their best to-day, and the old town appears to advantage. On one occasion I observe a young man kiss a male relative or friend, one of a party he encounters in the street; but this is the only instance of kissing among men I have seen as yet during my travels in France. I fancy the custom is either going out, or has never existed to the extent asserted by some travellers.

On the principle, I suppose, of "better late than never," the people of Falaise have recently erected an equestrian statue to William the Conqueror in the Place Trinité. It is a fine piece of workmanship, and looks well enough.

Whenever I remain on Sunday anywhere during my travels, I always think that one's comfort is a good deal promoted by the kind of hotel I happen to be stopping at. I ought not, therefore, to quit Falaise without bearing my humble testimony to the quiet homeliness and civility which prevail at the Hôtel de Normandie. It is a most pleasant resting-place.

Before leaving the more beaten track of Calvados I would observe, that the country about

Caen, Bayeux, and Falaise, is by no means so beautiful or picturesque as that of the other portion of this department, or of the other departments. The London and Brighton Railway Company are quite right when they advertise "the picturesque route to Paris;" but the reader who would wish to see the finest parts of Normandy, should deviate with me from the beaten track. I was much disappointed myself with the description of Calvados given by Mr. Musgrave. The reality, I thought, fell short of it. He speaks particularly of fine velvety turf—a great luxury to the pedestrian—to be found along the roads between Caen and Bayeux, and Caen and Falaise. Now it may have appeared so to the reverend gentleman seated on the diligence, or in a *voiture*, but to me walking it was quite otherwise. I found the turf by the side of the roads stony and gritty, and intersected now and then with ruts to draw off the water. I am sorry to be so prosaic, but in the course of my humble travels I would wish to describe things as I find them, and not to mislead the reader by poetic descriptions.

Monday, Sept. 14th.—I left Falaise early this morning for Argentan, distant twenty-two kilomètres (or thirteen miles). I stopped at a village inn, and had some breakfast of coffee and bread and butter. The landlord was quite drunk. His wife made matters worse by attempting to shut him up in an adjoining room; but he rushed out again, and was inclined to be obstreperous. He, however, showed me the attention of bringing a clean napkin. I was amused at the fidelity of mine host's dog. It seemed at first disposed to be fierce, but became calm on his master saying with reference to me, "A friend." The faithful animal, however, kept between me and his master all the time, with eyes fixed on my every movement, as if prepared to spring, and conscious of his owner's need of protection and utter helplessness in the case of attack on the part of the stranger. The landlord insisted on sitting by my side, and was so incoherent in his talk, and unpleasant to witness, that I disposed of the meal as quickly as possible, paid my reckoning, and departed. I put my host in some good humour by our exchanging drinks, he putting his glass of cider to my cup of coffee. On getting a short distance from the inn, I sat down on a bank by the wayside, quite discomfited at this morning's adventure. The inn was clean and comfortable, and more than usually civilized for one by the road-side—witness the napkin—and yet all was marred by the landlord's drunken propensities. I pitied the wife, who seemed a quiet, respectable woman, though she wanted judgment in the mode of dealing with her husband. What surprised me much was, how this man could thus early in the morning be drunk, unless he had a very weak head, or had been drinking all night, or was never quite sober. He was drinking weak-looking cider out of a small glass.

An imperial road leads from Falaise to Argentan. Shortly after quitting Falaise, you pass out of the department of Calvados into that of Orne. Between Falaise and Argentan there are only small villages all the way. The country, however, is very beautiful in parts. For several miles before reaching Argentan, the church of St. Germain presents an imposing appearance, towering as it does above the other buildings. At length the town itself is seen as you approach, presenting a close compact aspect. On arriving at Argentan, I entered the church of St. Martin, at the entrance of the town.

There are some old painted glass windows here, and the chandeliers to light the church seemed to me elegant and in good taste. I observe a semi-castellated castle or tower, and then enter the church of St. Germain, which also has some painted glass windows. This is a very fine church. I put up at the Hôtel des Trois Maries. One advantage which the pedestrian traveller has is, that he is enabled *en route* often to see the principal lions of the place, while the railway traveller on reaching his hotel is in a state of mist as to the kind of town he has reached.

At Argentan there are two curious-looking clocks, suspended midway across the street, one near the church of St Germain. The device appears new, and is certainly striking. After the *table d'hôte* dinner, I walked through the town to the river Orne, where there are some baths. Altogether the town of Argentan, which is the chief place of the canton, is of good size and very clean-looking, at the same time preserving an antique appearance interesting to the stranger.

Tuesday, Sept. 15th.—This morning I left Argentan with uncertainty as to where I should take up my quarters at night. The first stage I reached was Écouché, a canton town, eight kilomètres (or five miles) from Argentan. Here I stopped to breakfast, and afterwards visited the church, an interesting edifice. Part of it is covered with a wooden roof, apparently very old. Then on through Flormentel to Briouze, also a canton town, eighteen kilomètres (or eleven miles), where I halted, and had a half bottle of cider and some cakes at the Hôtel de la Poste. Then on again to Flers, seventeen kilomètres (or ten miles), where I put up at the Hôtel d'Ouest, a very good inn. The road is imperial all the way.

I found the long walk to-day very dusty, and the cordonniers, who were brushing the roads, would not condescend to stop as you passed. The scenery in parts is fine, but again either barren or shut out by hedges and trees. Flers is a modern-built canton town of good size, containing a great many hotels, and apparently rising in importance, no doubt on account of the railway in progress through it. There is an old church and a chapel, and a new church in the course of erection, which is a conspicuous object in and near the town.

Wednesday, Sept. 16th. — I walked this morning from Flers to Tinchebray, fourteen kilomètres (or eight miles). I joined the *table d'hôte* dinner at the hotel there, at twelve o'clock, by way of breakfast. About half a dozen of us, all men, sat down to dinner at this primitive hour. Tinchebray is an old-fashioned canton town, yet not bearing so antique an appearance as many others in Normandy of similar size. The church is extremely old and curious-looking. The town is prettily situated in a valley, surrounded by hills covered with trees and foliage.

As the reader of history will remember, Tinchebray was the scene of a battle, in 1106, between Henry I. and his eldest brother Robert, Duke of Normandy, in which the former was victorious. Though this battle is uneventful in our country's annals, as if the result had been different it would not have interfered with the steady march of national events, yet the victory was all-important to the chiefs concerned. To Henry it rendered secure the throne of England, while Robert it consigned to a dreary dungeon, where he lingered on in hopeless captivity during the long remainder of his life—if

I recollect rightly, twenty-eight years. Such, alas! was the conduct of the King of England to his brother.

From Tinchebray I walked this afternoon to Vire, sixteen kilomètres (or ten miles), and arrived there, I put up at the Hôtel St. Pierre. It is an imperial road from Flers to Vire. The scenery on the way is in parts fine, but by no means very striking anywhere. Shortly after leaving Tinchebray you quit the department of Orne, and re-enter that of Calvados.

Thursday, Sept. 17th.—I took a walk this morning about Vire, before the *table d'hôte* breakfast, at ten o'clock. I saw the church of Notre Dame. The exterior is very plain and simple, but the interior is fine though rather florid, the pillars of the choir being painted in various colours. Near the church there are two or three very old houses of wood. There is another church at Vire, and one in the course of erection.

Near the church of Notre Dame I saw a coffin lying in state, in a recess, apparently at the undertaker's. Candles were placed at the head of the coffin, though not lighted. A lantern, however, apparently was lighted. A young girl, in deep mourning, closely veiled, and seemingly the chief mourner, was seated near the corpse. At the foot of the coffin was a basin containing holy water and a sprig of myrtle. Each person who passed at least took off his hat, or, in the case of a woman, courtesied and crossed herself. Some sprinkled the coffin with holy water, either with the hand or from the myrtle sprig.

Vire is celebrated for its walks. I strolled along part of them. They are not, however, kept in good order, and are without seats. I presume they are not much appreciated or used by the inhabitants. Near the walks are the ruins of the castle. From the grounds here a very good view is obtained, on one side, of the town, with a pretty water-mill below; and on the other, of the suburbs and the valley of the Vire.

I found the Hôtel St. Pierre thoroughly homely and comfortable. When the *table d'hôte* breakfast had progressed some time, a priest and his friend arrived, and they were informed, I could hear, as a great fact, that there was an Englishman at the table. "What! marching!" said the priest. "Yes." Presently my friend, an elderly and most pleasant-looking man, appeared, smiling to all around; but we did not meet to have any conversation. When I received the bill, I discovered one or two items which had been increased, but the charges, or, if you may term them, overcharges, were so little, as to cause more amusement than annoyance. The Hôtel St. Pierre is beautifully situated on the road to Avranches. On taking my departure, the whole household assembled at the entrance to wish me a good voyage. My host's daughter, a nice-looking girl, asked me to recommend the hotel to my friends in England. I promised to do so, a promise which I now gladly fulfil, for I look upon you, dear readers, as among my best friends.

CHAPTER VI.

Rich scenery—Torigny—A Sister of Mercy—Hôtel d'Angleterre —Interested fellow-travellers—St. Lo—Table d'hôte at Hôtel Soleil Levant—Brother Pedestrians—Description of town of St. Lo—Road to Coutances—Marigny—Coutances—Hôtel d'Angleterre again—The Cathedral—Church of St. Pierre— St. Nicholas—Public garden—Bréhal—Cider in a cup—A sale by auction—Dust—Granville—Hôtel du Nord—A wet day—Visit to the church—The lower town—General aspect of the place—A storm-signal—Sartilly—A courteous stranger— The valley of Sartilly—The return from market—Pont Callant—A delightful view—Avranches—Hôtel de France— Shut up in the public garden—My escape—A contrast.

Thursday, Sept. 17th (continued).—I left Vire—which, I may observe, is the chief place of the arrondissement—at about twelve o'clock to-day for Torigny. For about three miles after leaving Vire, the scenery throughout the valley is most rich and beautiful. Orchards, too, are passed, ripe with apples, and giving forth a sweet scent. Then the scene changes, and for two or three miles there is nothing particular;

but again the scenery becomes very fine, with some rock in places. From the bridge over the Vire, especially, a grand view right and left is obtained. Here commences a steep hill, gradually ascending from the valley for a mile or two. Near the top of this hill a panoramic scene is displayed of all the country below for many miles, and is very magnificent. Afterwards, until Torigny, the scenery continues rural and pleasant. Altogether, the country walked over to-day between Vire and Torigny has presented the best scenery I have yet seen in Normandy. Indeed, so much so, as to be at times and places almost overpowering by its beauty and grandeur.

The distance between Vire and Torigny is twenty-five kilomètres (or fifteen miles). I did not reach my destination until seven o'clock, as the road was hilly, and I had lingered much and long to enjoy the beautiful views before and around me, and which the fineness of the weather rendered the more charming. It was dusk as I entered the canton town of Torigny. It is a good-sized place, situated on a large lake, along the banks of which, on one side, is a splendid row of pine-trees, forming a fine walk, with seats. The only promenader I see now in the twilight is a sister of mercy from the adjoining convent, whose grim, dark-looking walls rise up like those of a prison before the beholder. Her sacred habit and profession render this young girl, though alone at night, quite safe from any attack or annoyance on the part of the rude, the gay, or the dissolute. Moreover, her calling places her character above all suspicion, and enables her to take an evening walk here, among the seclusion of these trees, free from the intrusive gaze of the vulgar, or the impertinent scrutiny of the curious.

I looked at the church at Torigny, which, however, is a very plain edifice. I put up at the Hôtel d'Angleterre, a comfortable and unpretending inn. There were two commercial travellers in the *salle à manger*, with whom I entered into some conversation. They were much interested with my travels, and particularly pleased to hear that I was so much delighted with the scenery I had witnessed today. Frequent communion with it had not, in this case at least, diminished their appreciation of the glory and magnificence of the landscape. I may here remark that, shortly after crossing the bridge over the Vire, you pass out of the department of Calvados into that of Manche. It is an imperial road from Vire to Torigny.

Friday, Sept. 18*th.*—I left Torigny at seven o'clock this morning for St. Lo. The distance along an imperial road is thirteen kilomètres (or eight miles). The way is hilly, and there is nothing particular in the scenery. I joined the *table d'hôte* breakfast at ten o'clock at the Hôtel Soleil Levant, which was good and well served. Mine host mentioned, as a fact likely to interest me, that two young gentlemen walking had just left the inn. I had, indeed, as I told him, observed them leaving the town. Though the country is so well suited for the pedestrian traveller, I see very few of them about anywhere, either doing the whole or part of their journey on foot.

St. Lo is the chief place or capital of the department of Manche; it is a modern-looking town. The Hôtel de Ville, a new structure, and the Palais de Justice, are fine buildings. The church, with its two towers, has an imposing aspect as to the exterior, but inside it is extremely plain and simple. The church of St. Croix has been, I presume, pulled down, as a fine new church in the Place St.

Croix is nearly finished, and probably occupies the site of the old edifice. There are two very ancient houses of wood in the Rue des Poids National which are deserving of notice.

Much as I approve of the "thorough" in pedestrianism, my mettle was sorely tried to-day on the walk along the imperial road from St. Lo to Coutances, a distance of twenty-nine kilomètres (or eighteen miles). The road was very dusty, the weather dry and hot, and the walk was unenlivened by any scenery. Moreover, even the country round, such as it is, was shut out from view generally by high thick-set hedges. I passed through the canton town of Marigny; but, with this exception, there are only villages between the two places. On arriving at Coutances in the evening, I took up my quarters at the Hôtel d'Angleterre.

Saturday, Sept. 19th.—I walked about the town of Coutances this morning before the *table d'hôte* breakfast. It is the chief place of the arrondissement. I saw the cathedral. The exterior, consisting of three towers, is very striking, especially from a distance. The inside, though plain, is very chaste and beautiful. I also inspected the church of St. Pierre. The two towers are extremely elegant, and the painted glass in the interior is very fine. I also entered the church of St. Nicholas, which, however, is a very plain edifice. I walked in the public garden, which is the gift of a townsman, to whom a monument has been deservedly erected here. A munificent gift indeed! These gardens, though small in actual space, are very beautiful; well stocked with flowers, and kept in excellent order, with good seats liberally placed. There is a kind of labyrinth at one end of the garden, and though its perplexities are rather unmeaning and absurd, yet it looks pretty, and from the smooth gravel top a good view is obtained of the country round, and especially of the cathedral. Coutances, though wearing a somewhat modern aspect, contains particularly narrow streets, and stands rather apart—not, on the one hand, bearing the antique appearance of the Norman town, nor, on the other, the convenient size and appearance of the modern-built town. It is situated on a hill, and, as seen from the road leading out of Coutances to Granville, reminds one of the saying of Scripture, that "a city which is built on a hill cannot be hid."

After breakfast I left Coutances, and this day walked to Granville, a distance of twenty-nine kilomètres (or eighteen miles) along the imperial road. It is not a pleasant walk, there is no scenery. On the way to Granville I passed through Bréhal, a canton town, small, and not of so much importance as others of the like kind I have seen. I stopped at an inn there, and asked for a half bottle of cider, and was served with it for the first time in a cup. It was very good cider, and only ten cents.

At Bréhal there was an auction going forward. A common kind of fellow stood on a table, and announced some earthenware jugs for sale. He proceeded in a very matter-of-fact kind of way, and without the well-known laudatory preface of the article so familiar an accompaniment of the English auction. Perhaps, however, in this instance it may have been unnecessary. It was a pitiable spectacle—I presume a seizure for rent; such, indeed, as one often hears and reads of in England, but which, as a fact, I had never witnessed. The ordinary traveller who proceeds through a country in these civilized times lives at sumptuous hotels, and passes from place to place in splendid railway carriages. Though he may not possess the indifference of the luxurious traveller depicted by Sterne, who goes from capital to capital without looking aside to the right hand or the left, yet, however much he uses his eyes, he sees things, if I may use the expression with reverence, "through a glass darkly," while the pedestrian meets the people he visits "face to face." It was a humble cottage before which this auction was taking place. All the articles of furniture and domestic use had been taken out—tables, chairs, bedstead, bed, pots, pans, kettle, cups, saucers, and other things—and were strewed about on the road. A small knot of persons, evidently neighbours and friends, from their downcast, sorrowful countenances, were standing around and about. I could not discover the occupants of the cottage amid the crowd. Probably they were not there to see their household goods so ruthlessly dispersed. Possibly they are some ne'er-to-do-well couple, who, in spite of their extravagance, have won, if not the esteem, at least the affection of their neighbours. No doubt each article was well enough known to these people, hence there was no need to particularize it. After two or three bids the earthenware jugs were finally knocked down, or rather awarded, for there was no hammer, for a few sous. Then the next article was put up, and the same process repeated; and so on. A respectably-dressed man seemed to have the general conduct of the sale. He stood near the table on which was the humble auctioneer, and wrote down the articles, and prices for which the same sold, in a book. I presume, therefore, that the calling of auctioneer does not stand so well in France as in England, and that his duties, at least on an occasion like the present, are considered rather ignominious than otherwise. One thing there was which could not fail to impress the stranger, and that was the respect for law and order which prevailed, though the process here enacted was calculated beyond measure to harass and exasperate the feelings, if not rouse sensations almost amounting to frenzy. Yet there was no policeman or gendarme near. These two functionaries might have been easily seized by the crowd, and bundled out of the town, as they say in the common tongue; yet they remained untouched. Though unarmed even themselves, they quietly and fearlessly did their painful duty with as much composure as if supported by a regiment of soldiers. They feared no harm, for in them was represented the majesty and power of the law.

On entering Granville, I was nearly blinded with the dust; it swept past me in regular clouds. I presume, however, that the good people here are too much accustomed to this visitation to entertain any thoughts of removing it by water-carts, for on turning back on one occasion I was surprised to see a party of well-dressed ladies and gentlemen standing quietly in the middle of the road, and engaged in animated conversation as composedly as if they had been in a drawing-room, though the dust regularly enveloped them in its white folds. Granville is built on a hill and in the valley below. You enter through a romantic fissure in the rock to the sea-shore and the baths. Then there is the harbour and the pier. The church is situated on the hill, where also is the fort. There are two or three good streets. I put up at the Hôtel du Nord.

Sunday, Sept. 20th.—I breakfasted at a café near the hotel. It was a very wet morning, and up to the afternoon. During the latter part of the day I explored the town. I visited the church on the hill; it has some fine recently-painted glass windows, and altogether is a more pleasing edifice than most of the Norman churches I have yet seen, which are not known to fame. I stayed for the afternoon service, and remained through the whole of it. I never remember being present during a complete service in a Roman Catholic church before. I was seated in a chair just outside the railings of the high altar, so I had a good opportunity of observing what was going forward. The ceremonies seemed to me very unmeaning and absurd, and more worthy of a heathen temple than of a church dedicated to the purposes of Christian worship. There was, however, a certain degree of solemnity and awe about the proceedings calculated to impress the vulgar mind. After the service I mounted a small eminence in the churchyard, from which a good view is obtained of the lower part of the town and of the harbour.

Then I walked along the outside of the hill, and down near the baths and reading-room, on to the sands. The bathing was apparently over for the season. Then to the pier, from which there is a fine view of the whole place. The best houses and all the hotels are in the lower town. There is also a very small church or chapel there; I entered it in the morning during the service, and it was very crowded. There is need of a good church in this part of the town, that on the height being too distant, and perhaps, also, already too much occupied, for the people here to attend with comfort. There is also a chapel at the fort.

Granville is nominally only a canton town, though, like many other similar places, it has assumed an importance far beyond its municipal position. Granville has become a sea-side place of much resort. Though I saw the town amid the disadvantages of rain—and a rainy Sunday too—I was much pleased with the general aspect of the place. There are good sands for bathing, a fine pier for walking, and many characteristics calculated to attract the stranger. Steamers ply regularly between this place and St. Helier's, Jersey; consequently many English people, visitors to the Channel Islands, cross over here, stay two or three days, and then return. Probably many of them have never crossed the channel, and take this opportunity of just paying a visit to the French country. There is a steamer this very morning advertised to sail for Jersey, but Admiral Fitzroy, somehow or other, has transmitted the intelligence that there is a storm in the channel; so the signal is run up, and the vessel does not start. I see her in the harbour quite deserted by captain and crew, who, no doubt, are enjoying themselves in the town, thanks to the invention of storm-signals. About half a dozen people at the hotel are weather-bound, and made Sabbath observers against their will. However, they could not well be detained in a better or more comfortable inn. The Hôtel du Nord is a very large establishment, and one of the best in Normandy. The people are extremely civil, and the charges most moderate. You can live here, joining the two *tables d'hôte*, breakfast and dinner, for eight francs a day. The dinner was particularly good, and well served.

Monday, Sept. 21st.—The storm-signal is still up, and the waiting-maid is rallying two young men on the subject, and that they will not be able to leave for Jersey before Thursday. But the pedestrian is not bound by storm-signals, and therefore, though the weather is threatening, I quit my moorings early this morning. I am bound for Avranches, along the imperial road, a distance of twenty-six kilomètres (or sixteen miles). I took breakfast at a humble inn at Sartilly, about fifteen kilomètres (or nine miles) from Granville. It is a small canton town, with a plain church. I met a young Frenchman, apparently a commercial traveller, at the inn, who proposed to drive me in his *voiture* to a village at some distance, and at five o'clock on to Avranches; but I declined the offer, as it would take me out of my route. In order to show this, I took out my map, and pointed to him the position of the different places. He seemed surprised and delighted at the idea of a stranger possessing so much knowledge of localities as yet unvisited, and expressed himself strongly as to the convenience of a map. It certainly places you very much on a par with the natives as regards the topography of the country, if it does not give one a positive advantage over them.

Having parted from my friend, I left Sartilly, and proceeded on my way. The scenery is nothing in particular between Granville and Sartilly, but a fine avenue of poplars, shortly before entering the latter town, is worthy of notice. The valley of Sartilly is pretty and romantic, and shortly afterwards you see the Mont St. Michel and the neighbouring island of Tombeleine, and then a little further on the town of Avranches, though distant five miles.

From the number of persons with cattle on the road, it was apparently market-day at Avranches. I threaded my way on to the town through a succession of the peasantry, with horses, colts, oxen, sheep, and pigs, being driven, poked, beaten, coaxed, and dragged along in a variety of ways; but though unsold and homeward bound, they seemed as obstinate as possible. One man was carrying a small pig in a large bag on his shoulders as the best and shortest course. Beyond surprising the passers-by with squeaks coming from some unknown quarter, the animal was thus rendered incapable of further interfering with the laws of motion.

The scenery between Sartilly and Pont Callant, a kind of suburb of Avranches, is quiet and unobservable, but on ascending the hill, you begin to look upon a scene delightful and pleasing, until, on reaching the mound at the top, the view, with Mont St. Michel in the distance, becomes truly magnificent, though the absence of rock and, with the exception of the small river, of water, renders the immense expanse of green landscape somewhat monotonous after being looked upon for a short time. The weather all the way was wet and stormy, but a glimpse of sunshine on reaching Avranches rendered the view good, though on a fine sunshiny day it would be much better.

I walked in the public garden, and observed the statue here to General Valhubert, who was killed at the battle of Austerlitz. I traversed the streets in various directions. Avranches, which is the chief place of the arrondissement, is a much more modern-looking town than I had been led to expect. The houses do not look so quaint or old as in many other towns. There are no good streets, and few fine shops. Some of the ramparts remain, and a walk along the outskirts, with seats, affords fine opportunities for seeing the views. I entered the church, which, though a long building, is extremely plain in appearance. There is a marble slab erected by the Marquis de Belbeuf in 1844 to the memory of his predecessor of that name, the last bishop of Avranches, and who, it is stated, died and was buried at Hampstead, in England.

I took up my quarters at the Hôtel de France, and after dinner I again walked in the public garden. Here, while sauntering about until after dark, on going to the gates, I found them, to my surprise, shut and locked up for the night. No one apparently was suspected of being left behind. This was a dilemma. Of course, as the gates are near a main thoroughfare, there should have been no difficulty in getting out again. But the French are not a practical people. Many passed, and observed, and spoke to me, but did nothing. One asked whether I was shut in, a question which admitted of a self-evident answer. Another observed with composure that he presumed I should have to remain there all night. Again, I was told that I could not possibly scale the high gates—a fact of which, from reconnoitring them, I had become painfully aware. I inquired of another where the porter who had the keys lived, and was told there, pointing in the direction. I asked another whether the porter might not be sent for; he didn't know; another thought not, and another shook his head and passed on. At length a boy made his appearance, and I asked if he would fetch the custodian of the keys. He hesitated; I offered to give him something; still he hesitated, and went not. So finding matters becoming desperate, I left the great gates and walked round the garden, anxiously looking out for some way of escape. But high iron railings alone for a time met my view. At last I discover a vulnerable point in these fortifications. There are even here two sets of rails, and one very high, but neither quite inaccessible to the climber. I succeeded in getting out by means of climbing over both of them, though not without imminent risk of being spiked. This place was at the extreme end of the garden, and, on walking round to the great gates, I saw an old woman with a lantern groping about in the garden looking for the stranger, accompanied by the boy who seems to have repented and gone for her. I indicated to them that I had escaped, but gave the boy nothing, as I thought he deserved nothing, for the uncertainty and procrastination, and I presume he entertained the same view, as he did not ask for anything. I then adjourned to a café, which, however, is by no means so well fitted up as others I have entered. Here I was unexpectedly the observed of all observers. Two or three of the men looked as much astonished as if they were seeing a ghost. I presume, therefore, these are among those who so kindly passed me by. One of them, indeed, asked me how I got out, and on my telling him, he seemed much surprised. There was evidently an idea that the garden was so fortified that there was no escape. Presently the busy waiter caught up the news, and, on bringing the coffee, asked if I was the gentleman who had been shut up in the garden.

I mention this incident thus in detail, in order to give a practical example of the value of French politeness. There was no rudeness, no jeering at my mishap; no desire, I believe, that I should spend the night in the garden; but, on the contrary, I think a good deal of sympathy was felt for my forlorn condition. But still the trouble or exertion of fetching the key, or seeking out the custodian of it, and bringing her to the gate, was too great for a Frenchman to accomplish, at least for a stranger. As a contrast, I would mention what occurred the very first Sunday after my return to England. I was walking in the lawyers' gardens of the Temple, between the services, with an old friend of about eighty years of age. Presently a youth came up and said, "All out!" "What does he say?" my friend asks. I felt it necessary to translate, and replied, "He wishes to intimate that the time for closing the gardens has arrived." We accordingly made our way across the grass to an iron fence where there was a gate, which was, however, fastened. This to a gentleman of eighty was a reasonable impediment, so we were going to retrace our steps when the youth rushed forward, and without saying a word, slowly and with difficulty unwound the wire fastening, which served the purpose of lock and key, and let us out. We, of course, thanked him, but gave no gratuity, neither did he apparently expect any; it was a graceful act of practical courtesy from youth to age. Herein lies the contrast between the characteristics of the two countries. The Frenchman is all blandness and outward courtesy, but not ready to do anything practical. The Englishman is cold, discourteous, at times abrupt, and even rude, but ever willing, and indeed anxious, to lend a helping hand to friend, acquaintance, or stranger in any instance of real emergency, or where the circumstances of the case render such aid either desirable or necessary.

CHAPTER VII.

Avranches—Jardin des Plantes—Gateway of Chapel of St. George—Two churches—Museum—Court of Civil Tribunal—Stone, part of the old cathedral—A bath simple—The table d'hôte dinner—A new arrival—A profitable matter of inquiry—True French politeness—A deserted town—Fiction and travel—Village of Pont au Baud—Bad fare—A lift—Treacherous sands—Distant view of Mont St. Michel—A dangerous ford—Mont St. Michel—An indolent guide—Reception at the castle—The cloisters—Church—Dining-hall—Dungeons—A military salute—The workrooms—Dormitories—College and council chamber—The last to leave—Road to Pont d'Orson—Its wretched condition—A good-natured driver—Large families—Pont d'Orson—The church—Distance from Avranches—Hôtel de la Poste—A comfortable café—A literary girl.

Tuesday, Sept. 22nd.—It was a thorough wet day, the rain at intervals coming down in torrents. The streets, either in the middle or on both sides, were running in small brooks, requiring a regular jump to cross over. Avranches, situated on an incline, must be well drained by these periodic washings of nature. Before breakfast, and again in the afternoon, I walked in the Jardin des Plantes. The fog and mist most materially interfered with the prospect. I should say that the view from the top of the mound, under the Sous-Préfecture, is, on the whole, the grandest and finest; but, certainly, the Mont St. Michel is seen from the Jardin des Plantes more clearly and distinctly.

The Jardin des Plantes, from the small number of plants, hardly deserves the latter title; but it makes a very good promenade, and is well provided with seats. In this garden is erected the gateway of the chapel of St. George, constructed at Bouillet in the eleventh century, and removed and placed here by the Archæological Society in 1844. It is a very simple piece of architecture, and, beyond its antiquity, presents no particular features of interest.

I entered two other churches, being, with the principle one, apparently the only churches here. These two are close near to one another. One of them is very plain, but the other contains granite pillars, and is a good specimen of a Norman parish church.

After breakfast I visited the museum, which

contains some antiquities, and a small collection of paintings by French, or perhaps only Norman artists, with two or three attributed, though I should be inclined to think erroneously, to the old masters, especially the one said to be by Rubens. The museum is hardly worth visiting by the stranger, unless he has plenty of time. Underneath is the court of the Civil Tribunal, an elegant chamber with a beautiful groined roof. The public library is not here, but at the Hôtel de Ville. It was not, however, open, so I did not enjoy the opportunity of inspecting the collection of books.

I observed the stone enclosed by an iron chain at the Place Huet, on the top of the mound near the Sous-Préfecture. The inscription is to this effect, that the stone forms part of the entrance of the cathedral of Avranches, near which Henry II., King of England and Duke of Normandy, knelt to receive absolution from the Pope's legates for the murder of Thomas à Becket, Archbishop of Canterbury. In the course of the day I took a bath simple, which cost eighty cents. The bath-room was of good size and airy, and the water clean.

We assembled at the *table d'hôte* dinner, at

the Hôtel de France, only few in number to-day. When we had nearly finished, a *voiture* drove up the yard in front of the *salle à manger*, containing a well-known London professor and his wife. He was driving himself, a most sensible mode of proceeding through the country when accompanied by a lady, or unable or disinclined to walk. By the way, how comes it to pass that at young ladies' schools so little progress is made in the study (or acquisition rather, which is the term used there) of French, that it becomes necessary to use the fingers in aid of speech while travelling? For instance, this lady just arrived, elegant, accomplished, and well-connected, I observe availing herself of such assistance, in order to make mine hostess comprehend that she wishes to go to her room for five minutes before coming down to dinner. I think such a subject might form a useful, if not profitable, matter of inquiry or discussion for those of my readers who pay two or three hundred a year in order to have the dear girls educated at some fashionable and expensive school in London or at Brighton. Presently the newly-arrived guests make their appearance, and my host eyes them, as well he might, with evident satisfaction. His true French politeness much impressed me, for he never left the table for a moment, though, under the circumstances, he might well have been excused for doing so, particularly as we had no lady among ourselves. But the sacred rule of hospitality was made to override that of paying attention to a new arrival. I am surprised that the long drive has not rendered the learned professor impervious to any kind of drink; but, in fact, he lingers long over the carte, and is asking his wife, who probably had travelled on the continent in her maiden days, about some particular wine with great earnestness. "Is it good?" "Are you sure?" "Have you tried it?" Poor man! There was, no doubt, cause for such anxiety, for he has since passed away from the scene of his active, honourable, and lucrative labours.

Avranches is a place much resorted to by the English, and I was informed by the man who showed me over the museum that there are many of my countrymen living here now. The town, however, is quite deserted to-day on account of the rain, and appears forlorn enough. I walk up and down the principal street, almost the only person out, and until I attract unpleasant attention to myself from persons looking out of windows or standing on door-steps. But a place always presents to the pedestrian, moving along without sojourning anywhere, an appearance more or less accidental, more temporary than permanent. Avranches to me, visiting it in rain and tempest, is a dull, gloomy, lifeless sort of place; but I see many nice villas in the suburbs, and can well imagine that in fine weather Avranches presents a cheerful, happy, and animated aspect, and that many of my fair countrywomen would be met with walking, riding, and driving hereabouts. And to judge also from my hotel bill, I should think living here to be very economical.

I think Avranches, from the descriptions, must be the place where the accomplished author of "Life in Normandy" lived. It is a great pity that he did not relate simply his own experiences, instead of mixing up the real with the imaginary. Fiction is one thing, and travel another; but to attempt to combine the two I believe to be a mistake. Still, I am reminded by this book how little a casual visitor to a place learns of the mode of life of the inhabitants. For in my case there is no Angelica or

Angelina—her exact name matters little, as the girl is purely imaginary—to accompany me, with her little brothers, to the sea-side, and show how sand-eels are caught. Life in one place is more real, though the faculty is rare to portray it with fidelity and truth.

Wednesday, Sept. 23rd.—I left Avranches this morning, *en route* for Mont St. Michel. It was raining drizzly, but soon cleared up, and the weather became moderately fine. I walk along the imperial road, and pass through the village of Pont au Baud, where there is a bridge over the river Selune. I went into the church here, which, however, is a very plain building. From thence to some cross-roads, where there is a road-side inn. Here I stopped to have some breakfast of bread and butter and coffee without milk—bad, and very dear, and long in coming. I entered the kitchen to see what I could do myself, but the good woman resented such interference. She seemed more interested in the arrival just then by a dray-cart of a barrel of brandy, the quality of which she tasted in true scientific fashion, the man boring a hole, and obtaining a small glassful in this way, and afterwards driving in a peg. The good woman first promised me some milk, but afterwards said it was too bad to drink. I did not reason with her as to the inconsistency, but strongly suspected that at this inn this morning milk, either good or bad, had no existence except in my hostess's imagination.

Then on again for some distance, when I took a turning to the right, by a road of grand communication, which leads to the sea-shore. There is a like road opposite, leading to the village of St. Aubin de Terregatte, which is not indicated on the map. A short way from the sands I accepted a lift in a *voiture*, containing a driver, and a French gentleman and his wife. I took my seat on the box, and proceeded with them to Mont St. Michel. The road along the sea-shore is very bad; we walked a good deal of the way; over the sands it is a little better. The pedestrian should on no account allow himself to be tempted to leave the carriage-track, and trust himself to the treacherous sands, which look at low water smooth, beautiful, and firm. The dangers of the sands around Mont St. Michel have no doubt been much exaggerated by travellers, but still I think they exist. In times gone by fatal accidents have, I believe, occurred here. The driver warned the French gentleman, who was walking a little on one side on some untrodden sand, that there was danger in doing so. The *voiture* track makes a wide sweep round, instead of taking a direct course; and the inhabitants of Mont St. Michel evidently have some idea on the subject, for the route they take to the mainland is very circuitous, and in places going through pools of water, instead of over the dry and more tempting sand. It is supposed that the sands here are in places quick; that is, though in appearance solid or firm, yet in reality alive, and liable to give way at once on being trodden. If so, the unsuspecting traveller might, indeed, suddenly, in a moment, in the twinkling of an eye, meet with a terrible death. No grave, no funeral, not even the committal to the deep amid a solemn service; but a burial while yet alive, to be instantly followed by an awful death while buried; a sudden disappearance from this world's stage and its scenes of activity while full of health and strength, and unconscious of any sense of peril.

I think the best view of Mont St. Michel is to be obtained from the sands, as you approach the little rocky island. It rises above the level of the sea, and is seen unencumbered by the narrow street, and dirty houses. It looks more grand and magnificent at this moderate distance than on a more close inspection. We realize here some of that enchantment which distance is said to give to a view.

When we reached the Mont we found the water there still very deep, on account of the recent rains. A guide, half-stripped, took hold of the horse's head and led it through the water, which came over the carriage wheels, and thus we entered the Mont. The sea to-day never entirely left the Mont dry, but it would have been up to the middle to cross; but this may have been owing to the heavy rains of the last two or three days. Moreover, it may be now spring-tides. If I had been on foot I should certainly have encountered a difficulty in passing through the water near the Mont. I might have managed on the shoulders of one of the guides, or by some passing *voiture*, but I saw no boat, until about the time of our returning, by which I could have crossed or recrossed the narrow part of sea-water.

Mont St. Michel comprises the castle and

also a small town or village, consisting, for the most part, of one long street. There are three gateways, which are very near to each other. Near the second there are two cannons. There are two small inns and a little church or chapel. Some of the houses here and there are very old, but the majority of them are modern built, two or three forming pleasant dwellings. There is a walk along the ramparts affording a good view.

Several *voitures* had preceded ours to the Mont, and near the principal inn many visitors, French and English, were assembled. We soon formed a party, and under the self-appointed guidance of a stalwart woman, we started for the castle. Our guide did as little as was well possible. She walked before us with rapid strides, and then entered the chapel and stood by in silence, while we, in mute astonishment, looked around, and then at one another, as much as to inquire, "Do you see anything in particular?" for a plainer or more simple edifice, or one more devoid of ornament or matter of curiosity or interest of any kind, could not well be imagined. Then she collected her gratuities, pointed the way to the castle, and with as rapid strides descended to guide up some other party.

Arrived at the castle, we were received with much civility, though at first with some little ceremony. We entered our names and addresses in a book, and those of us who had permits gave them up. I, not being provided with this document, produced my passport, which was accepted as a substitute. Then we were conducted over the castle by a very civil and attentive soldier, guard or gendarme. It was then used as a prison, but I believe is so no longer. First we saw the cloisters, which are very fine, with small pillars elegantly worked. Then the church, which is newly built inside, though it contains some curious old figures in one or two of the side chapels, or rather recesses, apparently parts of the ancient church. The body of the building is used as a dining-hall for the prisoners, the choir alone being set apart for service. Then further to a place beyond the church, from which a good view is obtained. From thence into the kitchen, and then we ascended the church to nearly the top, in order to see the view. You can apparently ascend still higher, to the highest part of the church, but none of the party feeling inclined to do so, I did not ascend, as I should have been left behind.

Afterwards we descended to the dungeons where contumacious prisoners are confined. I entered one of them. It contained no furniture but a chain, to be used if necessary. The dungeon, however, was spacious, and had a window, giving some light. While passing through the passages near here, one of the prisoners, who was sweeping, shouldered the broom, and gave us a salute in military style. I touched my hat in return, and the poor man seemed quite moved by this simple act of courtesy. I could not help speculating as to his crime. He was a fine, handsome, and well-formed man, and had evidently not lost his sense of self-respect. It seemed humiliating to our common nature to reflect that such a man should sink so low as to be subjected to treatment more suitable for the beasts that perish. And yet probably had any of us, now proudly passing this man by, strong in the feeling of liberty and freedom from crime, been placed in similar circumstances of temptation, we should have fallen likewise.

We saw the prisoners at work, some at looms, and others making various articles, but all usefully employed. The workrooms are not well ventilated. An English lady declined to enter one of the rooms, saying to her friends while on the threshold, "Oh, I cannot stand this!" A French gentleman put his handkerchief to his nose. And yet such atmosphere it is the daily lot of the prisoners to breathe. What a dreadful fate! We inspected one of the dormitories. The beds were clean and separate. At about three o'clock, when the prisoners were gone to dinner, we entered the two large rooms formerly the college and council chamber. The college has small pillars and the chambers large ones, very much like those in the Temple Church. We also passed through dark passages and other places, and altogether were shown the place very thoroughly.

I then descended to the sea-shore. There were about a dozen *voitures* here to-day, some drawn by two horses, others by one. Gradually, with more or less of difficulty, they all departed except ours, which was the last to leave, either through the timidity of my friends or their driver, or from his wish to remain, or give his horse more rest. Curiously enough, I observed that the box seat I occupied was the only vacant one in all the vehicles—all besides were quite full, both inside and out. At last we started through the water, and, by the aid of many objurgations on the part of our Jehu to the poor horse, we safely crossed to the dry sands, but proceeded then with some danger, and were nearly jolted over once. Then we reach the departmental road to Pont d'Orson, which is in even a worse state. We proceed the nine kilomètres (or five miles) at a walking pace nearly all the way, the poor horse even then stopping two or three times of his own accord to rest. I never remember travelling by so bad a public road before, but the state is caused, no doubt, by the rain, as it has every appearance of being a good road in fine weather. Towards Pont d'Orson there was a cordonnier scraping the road, and he shook his head in despair at the labour, almost useless, he was performing. How I should have managed on foot along here I scarcely know. The road was impassable to the pedestrian. I must have threaded my way through the fields and commons, though even these were wet and soaky.

Our driver was a good-natured fellow, objurgatory, certainly, to the poor animal he drove, but still kind and forbearing. He kept up, too, a running commentary on men and things with his passengers. Once he asked one of a group of children, about six, whether they all belonged to the same family, to which a little maid replied, "Yes; and two others who are away." This answer highly amused him, for such a large family must be very rare in France. However, perhaps perceiving that the fact had no particular significance in my eyes, he related a story of an English family which two or three years before had stayed for a while at the Hôtel de France, at Avranches, from which he had come. There were eighteen children, and, with servants, amounted to nearly thirty persons, and occupied almost the whole hotel.

According to the old proverb, "'tis a long lane without a turning;" and even a bad road will come to an end; so, in course of time, we reach the canton town of Pont d'Orson. I part from my friends at their hotel, and proceed to inspect the place—as much, at least, as the twilight would permit. It is a good-sized town, but modern-built and looking. I entered the church. It presents a fine appearance. I could only dimly see the altar and figures in the north aisle. The distance by the direct road from Avranches to Pont d'Orson is twenty-two kilomètres (or thirteen miles). The *détour* by Mont St. Michel, of course, makes the route longer. I put up at the Hôtel de la Poste. After dinner, I adjourned to a most comfortable café opposite, where I wrote my notes. The people — a mother and daughters—were so homely and domestic, that I regretted I had not taken up my quarters here, for there seem to be bed-rooms. One of the young women, a pretty girl, is quite literary. She is sitting at a table by herself, with a good deal of manuscript before her, writing. What is it, I wonder? A novel, a poem, a play? Will it find a publisher? Will it succeed? Is she laying the foundation of literary fame, or merely producing something which will only end in disappointment and vexation? I long to ask her, but respect the privacy of the authoress. Presently two or three male acquaintances come in, but though they rally the girl on matters in general, they preserve silence as to the manuscript, and I forget my curiosity in admiration of their tact and feeling courtesy.

CHAPTER VIII.

A simple inscription—St. James—A funeral service—Hôtel St. Jacques—A case for sympathy—A cloth mill—St. Hilaire du Harcouet—The church there—Hôtel de la Croix Blanche—A liberal host—Mortain—Hôtel de la Poste—A severe rebuke— The cascades — The church—Voitures— Barenton—Out of Manche into Orne —A lift—An unexpected host—Domfront— Juvigny—Fair-day—A whirligig—A crowded inn—A new custom—A regular downpour—Villages of La Chapelle— Moche and Couterne—Enter department of Mayenne—Couptrain—An inhospitable inn—A ready mode of exit—Remarks on treatment of strangers—A walk by moonlight—Prez-en-Pail --Moderate charges—Suggestion to the pedestrian—Distance.

Thursday, Sept. 24th.—From Pont d'Orson I walked to St. James, a canton town, along a road of grand communication. The distance is fifteen kilomètres (or nine miles). It is a pleasant and rural walk. I passed a fine plantation of beech trees, and a villa prettily situated at the end of an avenue of trees. I was much struck with the simplicity of the following inscription in a country churchyard : "Ici

le corps de George Baron. Priez pour lui. 1858."
St. James is a modern town, situated on a hill, which overlooks a pretty valley. The church is a large plain building, in the course of being enlarged. There was a funeral service going forward, and from the number and respectability of the mourners, the deceased must have been some person of consequence. Near the church there is a chapel which was closed.

I had breakfast *à la fourchette* at the Hôtel St. Jacques. The position of the landlady excited my sympathies. The inn is newly established. I had been attracted to it by a framed placard I saw somewhere, giving a view of the place, otherwise, as it is situated a little on a cross-road outside the town, it would have esaped my observation. The hotel is too grand for a small canton town, and evidently does not answer. The good woman, when I came in, gave me that look of despair which a flicker of prosperity amid adverse circumstances so often produces. A very beautiful, fine young woman, probably her daughter, I overheard saying to her mother, "Perhaps the gentleman will stay the night;" but she only shook her head despairingly in reply. I had a great mind to verify the young woman's prediction concerning myself, but it was early in the day, I was not tired, and there is nothing to be seen here. Presently a stout burly man entered, and roughly asked the landlady whether I was the only guest. He gave one the impression of being someway, as landlord or agent, connected with the house. We two sat down to breakfast. The soup was almost the worst I have ever tasted, but the cider was the best I met with in the country. I parted from my hostess in the most friendly manner, and could not help pitying her as I walked away. My appearance had evidently disturbed her. I was that single swallow which, so far from betokening summer, only suggests the continuance of winter. It often happens that we can bear with better patience continued adversity, than those flickerings of better things which, when they disappear, render the darkness even greater than it was before.

I walked from St James, still along a road of grand communication, to St. Hilaire du Harcouet, a distance of twenty kilomètres (or twelve miles). The scenery is rural, and sometimes fine. Near St. Hilaire, to the left, there is a large cloth mill, prettily situated in a valley. On entering St. Hilaire there is a good public walk or enclosure, apparently recently set out, planted with chesnut trees, and having good granite seats. St Hilaire is a fine-looking modern canton town. The principal street runs along the imperial road you enter just before reaching the place; and there are other streets from the right and left, also along high-roads. A river flows through the lower part of the town, and is crossed by a bridge. The view on each side here, with mills on the left and a public washing-place, is very romantic.

The church at St. Hilaire is a large cathedral-like edifice recently built, but, as regards the east end and the towers, not finished. It contains nave, side-aisles, and choir, with noble granite pillars and painted windows. There is a tower of an old church on an eminence still remaining. From this spot there is a good view of the river and the verdure below. Beyond the east end of the church there is a fine boulevard with trees. The college and Hôtel de Ville are buildings worthy of observation.

There are two principal hotels at St. Hilaire, the Hôtel de la Poste and the Hôtel de France; but I was much attracted by the outward appearance of the Hôtel de la Croix Blanche, and that which is said so often to deceive, did not disappoint me in the present instance. The inn proved both clean and good. The bed-room was comfortable, spacious, and well furnished; and even an inkstand, with pens and ink, were provided there. We sat down to a very good *table d'hôte* dinner—mine host, two or three apparently commercial travellers, and myself. I presume the host has the credit of being a liberally-disposed man, for at the dessert there were some very fine peaches, which he handed to one of the guests, who declined to take any, remarking that he was sure the landlord must have given so much—I forget the sum—a-piece for them, and, though much pressed, he persisted in his refusal. I was not so self-denying, and in partaking of one of these excellent peaches reasoned thus: "If I, a stranger here, for the first and probably last time, do not eat one of these peaches, who is to do so? for clearly they will only remain good a short time, and will not serve, like medlars, as an ornament for dessert during a whole winter." I think, however, that such an innkeeper deserves encouragement, and I hope this account may induce some among my readers, who happen to wend their steps to St. Hilaire, to give the Hôtel de la Croix Blanche the preference. I cannot say anything in favour of the cafés here, which are very inferior, including the one I resorted to after dinner.

Friday, Sept. 25th.—I walk along the imperial road from St. Hilaire to Mortain, a distance of fifteen kilomètres (or nine miles.) It is very rural and pleasant all the way. There is a villa on the left, with a fine avenue of fir trees. To-day and yesterday I have observed by the roadside a good many sweet-chesnut trees. On coming near Mortain I saw, as a conspicuous object, a small church on a hill. I had some breakfast *à la fourchette* at the Hôtel de la Poste. Several things were brought to me by the landlord's daughter, a very pretty, well-dressed, ladylike girl, and *petite* in figure; but they were not good, and I was much dissatisfied with the meal; and probably only the circumstance of being so served restrained me from actually grumbling. However, I was destined to receive a severe rebuke. Presently the girl laid a cloth, and put some plates down at the further end of the table, and then a large tureen, and she and two young sisters sat down to a mid-day meal, without doubt their dinner. They drank cider; but what did that tureen contain? A hot tempting stew? No. Hear it, my Irish readers—only potatoes! I was surprised, and thought that this was only the first of several courses; but to my astonishment the meal began, continued, and ended with potatoes, and the sisters rose from their dinner apparently contented. What a contrast between my breakfast and their dinner!

There is nothing worth noticing in the town of Mortain itself, but it is beautifully situated, commanding a fine view of the surrounding country. It is the chief place of the arrondissement. I walked to the cascades, which were flowing probably more rapidly than usual, owing to the late rain. The view from here is very magnificent, including a good deal of rock. I saw over the church, a fine building, and observed the old portal. I could not distinctly discover the building of the Sous-Préfecture, where the old castle stood, unless it is the large building to the left at the entrance of the town.

Mortain owes any celebrity it possesses to the cascades, which are certainly worth going out of the way to visit. The water falls over the rocks in a very striking manner, and the whole spot is one where the solitary rambler would like to linger about for a day or two, if ample leisure afforded the time. There is an air of calm and serenity about the scene which is very charming.

On returning to the inn, my host's daughter asked me whether I had seen the view, and on my expressing delight at the prospect, she appeared much gratified. She did not at first comprehend my mode of travel. At dinner, she inquired where I was going. I replied to Domfront. "Oh!" she answered, shaking her head with an air of triumph, "there is no *voiture* going there to-day." I said I was going to walk there, which surprised her much. What a cab is to the Londoner, or a car to the Irish, so a *voiture* is to the French. A public or post conveyance, not rising to the importance of a diligence, is a *voiture*; again, any private or hired vehicle is equally a *voiture*. The constant application of this one word to so many different kinds of conveyance is frequently perplexing, and I am surprised that the French vocabulary in this respect has not received some addition.

I now proceed from Mortain to Barenton, a distance of ten kilomètres (or six miles) by the departmental road. It is a small and insignificant canton town, with a plain church. The scenery between the two places is good. Shortly after leaving Barenton there is a fine mansion to the left, situated in most beautiful grounds, with rocks and a waterfall. A short distance beyond Barenton I pass out of the department of Manche and re-enter that of Orne. The scenery continues fine; but latterly it was closed from view by the twilight. I am on the road to Domfront, distant from Barenton fifteen kilomètres (or nine miles), and still departmental. About six kilomètres (or four miles) from Domfront I accept a lift given me in a *voiture* containing a gentleman and a youth, probably his son, who is driving. We enter into conversation. Where am I going? To Alençon. Ah! I ought to have gone some other and shorter way. The French have no idea of a person simply walking to see the country. Do I know any hotel at Domfront? I answer no, and ask the gentleman which is the best hotel there. He replies, "The Hôtel de Commerce; that is mine." So it turns out my friend is an innkeeper, at which discovery we are both mutually amused. After some further remarks, he asks me whether I had ever been to Domfront before, and, on my replying in the negative, he appears relieved, which makes me suspect that the Hôtel de Commerce is not the best in the place; but, notwithstanding, I admire the man's answer and respect him for it. He has a perfect right to assume that his hotel is the best, or, at all events, the admission of proprietorship is quite sufficient to take away from me any grievance on this head if I am deceived.

We now approach Domfront, and, after crossing a river, enter the town. I can just see the church, which is a fine building. My landlord gets out at the foot of the hill, and, ascending by a shorter cut, is at the door of the Hôtel de Commerce when we arrive there, and ready to receive me with much formality. He ushers me into the inn, and introduces his wife, who directs the maid to show me to a good bedroom. On coming down-stairs, I had rather hoped to join the family circle; but mine host showed unmistakably that the equal relation of fellow-travellers had ceased, and that of host and guest had begun. He led the way to an inner room, a small *salle à manger*, where the cloth and things were laid, and then left me to be served by the waiting-maid in solitary state. Some hot soup soon appeared, followed by several excellent courses. I could not help reflecting on the possession of that tact on the part of the Frenchman which seemed to place him in a superior position to his brethren in England. He treated me with as much respect as if I had driven up in a *voiture*. But in my own country it too often happens that the meek and humble traveller is treated with disdain, and after waiting quietly for the unobtrusive meal, which he has ordered half an hour before, finds that it is forgotten.

Saturday, Sept. 26th.—On coming down this morning mine host was engaged, with coat off and his shirt sleeves up, in the menial occupation of skinning a hare. I walked out to see a little of Domfront before starting onward. It is a good-sized town, and the chief place of the arrondissement, but containing nothing remarkable. I observed two or three good hotels, and one in particular looking very stylish. There was, therefore, as I suspected, some motive in my landlord's question as to whether I had been here before; but I did not feel dissatisfied with the result of my survey of the town. If the Hôtel de Commerce be not the best hotel in the place, at any rate it is a very good one, and the charges are most moderate; and so if the reader should encounter mine host in a similar haphazard manner, he will, I think, have no occasion to regret the occurrence.

My host much persuaded me to take the public *voiture* in the afternoon for Alençon, and I found some difficulty in explaining to him my preference for walking. We parted with much friendliness, and I proceeded on my way. I had breakfast at Juvigny, a canton town containing a church with a fine spire. But before stopping for that purpose, I ascended the hill to where the better part of the town is situated, in order, if practicable, to find a better inn there than that by the roadside. There was a market or fair going on, and a crowd of people about buying and selling; but that which seemed principally to engross the attention of the public mind was a whirligig, such as you might see any day in England on a like occasion. It was elegantly fitted up with comfortable seats, and was taking round a number of children, and boys and girls, to the playing of a barrel organ and a drum. Round, round, round, until I became giddy looking at the machine, which has always seemed to me such a singular amusement. I believe that as a child I never entered one of them.

After all, the road-side inn proves the best in the place. It is said that first impressions are always important; and no doubt it is a great thing to be the first to attract the attention of the hungry or thirsty traveller. Besides, "it is the last ounce which breaks the camel's back." Many a weary traveller would prefer turning in at once to this inn by the wayside, than to make the toilsome ascent up the stiff bit of hill I have just come down. Hence, perhaps, no rival has attempted to interfere with the landlord's custom. A brisk trade he is doing to-day. The humble *salle à manger* is crowded. Here, there, and everywhere, the landlord and a dirty-looking maid are handing about portions of soup, tripe, meat, or vegetables; and cider and wine, though in moderate quantities, are plentifully called for. I take my place, and, what I only understood afterwards, a movement is made by the roughly-clad guests to shake hands; but to concentrate any attention on myself from the host or his servant, flying about in all directions, was a more difficult matter. At length I secure an audience of the maid, and ask her what I can have to eat. She replies, "A great many things;" so I order some soup. Then, once commenced, I attract my host's attention, which henceforth never flags. The customers around me have driven here from the country side, and one portion, of the cost of about four sous, or twopence, satisfies them; but I have been walking to a late breakfast, and am therefore a man of many courses. Presently, when I have to pay my reckoning, I produce a napoleon, at which the landlord looks as much startled as his brother in England would if I produced a ten-pound bank-note. Yet, surely, I think that the money he has been receiving this morning will suffice for change for a napoleon. But no; he goes to a chest of drawers, unlocks it, then finds his cash-box, and hands me the change in convenient pieces of gold and silver. On rising to depart the guests again made the movement to shake hands, which still I do not understand; but on reaching the road, the landlord, who had not noticed my exit, rushed out and made their meaning unmistakable. In his shirt-sleeves and with bare arms, he shook me by the hand in the most affectionate manner, as if we were about to have a fight then and there. But ours was merely the form of leave-taking after a brief acquaintance, which probably was rendered the more warm by the expenditure which a hungry appetite had rendered necessary. So it appears that here in this corner of Normandy there prevails a custom which, certainly, I have not found to exist elsewhere throughout the country.

After quitting my kindly host, in the midst of real sunshine, I had not proceeded far before a regular downpour of rain drove me to seek the friendly shelter of the neighbouring hedge. When the weather cleared up a little I walked onward. The scenery to-day is rural and pleasant. I pass through the villages of La Chapelle—Moche and Couterne. Near the latter place I enter the department of Mayenne. The way proves long and wearisome, and at nightfall I find myself quite out in the country. At length, late in the evening, I reach the small canton town of Couptrain. I enter the inn there, and ask an old woman I see for a bedroom. She shows me up-stairs, and into a large chamber with three beds. Am I to occupy this room alone? No. Then I prefer to take the single-bedded chamber adjoining, and request her to put it to rights, and to remove some apples on the table there. This she refuses, and says I must occupy the large chamber, which, under the circumstances, I thought most unreasonable and absurd; so I refused, and, much to the old dame's surprise, made my way down the dark stairs. Here I might easily have been placed in the ridiculous and not uncommon position of being compelled to ask the way out, instead of making a hasty and dignified retreat; for, on looking round, I could see dresser, pots, pans, fireplace, but where the door was seemed as difficult as the proverbial discovery of a pin in a bundle of hay. But luckily the landlord was just bidding good-bye to an acquaintance; and after the elaborate forms of politeness had been complied with usual among the French on such occasions, he opened the door, and, while host and guest were still engaged with their final adieus, I emerged into the street. I heard, or fancied I heard, a call to me from the inn, but I heeded it not. Perchance the old woman by this time had descended the stairs, and repented her rudeness to the traveller. Indeed, I never have occasion to resent any ill-treatment while travelling without some feeling of regret. The wrong-doer must, I am sure, bitterly regret the injury, and the more so as no redress is possible. The relative, friend, or acquaintance you offend you meet again; and though the annoyance may be too slight to call for any formal apology, yet a more friendly greeting, a warmer shake of the hand, a small favour granted unsolicited, will show by silent tokens that you admit yourself to have been in the wrong. But with the stranger the case is widely different. You and he meet, and part to meet never again. Therefore be kind to the stranger, and treat even his foibles with forbearance, for you will see his face again no more for ever.

The moon was shining splendidly, and, though very tired, I soon forgot my fatigue, especially as the night air gave me energy. In course of time I reached the canton town of Prez-en-Pail, and took up my quarters at an inn there, which was rough, but clean and comfortable. There was no pillow in my bed, but perhaps the omission may have been accidental, as the next morning I observed down-stairs through the opened door that there was such an important auxiliary to sleep in mine hostess's room. Prez-en-Pail is in the department of Mayenne, and even here, at this short distance from the Norman division of the country, there was a striking difference in the charges, they being more moderate. A pedestrian, therefore, who chose to walk through some of the unfrequented departments of France would find the living very cheap; but I am doubtful whether the scenery would be such as to repay the traveller. The road from Domfront to Prez-en-Pail is departmental all the way, and the distance is forty kilomètres (or twenty-four miles).

CHAPTER IX.

A fine village church—Wayside crosses—Out of Mayenne into Orne—St. Denis—Entrance to Alençon—A band playing—The cathedral—Hôtel Grand Cerf—Table d'hôte dinner there —Comments on travel—The public promenade—Cathedral again—Museum—Public library—Other buildings—A lift—Le Ménil Broux—An independent innkeeper—Le Mesle-sur-Sarthe—Mortagne-sur-Huine—The church—Hôtel de la Bouille—An uncivil landlady—A humble table d'hôte—A pretty but useless waiting-maid—A stroll after dinner—Mode of checking incivility at inns—St. Maurice—Out of Orne and re-enter Eure—Verneuil—Hôtel de la Poste—Passports.

Sunday, Sept. 27th.—I started from Prez-en-Pail this morning *en route* for Alençon. Here you fall into the imperial road from Mayenne to Alençon. The church at Prez-en-Pail, which I observe on leaving the place, is a new and large building. At the first village on the road there is a church with a fine tower having four windows. The interior also is worth inspecting. I pass three old wayside crosses, one on the left, and the two others on the right of the road. I also observe a small building containing a cross, being only the second of the kind I have seen in Normandy.

Some distance from Prez-en-Pail I quit the department of Mayenne and re-enter that of Orne. I pass through the village of St. Denis. There are rows of apple and pear trees by the road-side. The scenery is pretty good, though not striking. Alençon is distant from Prez-en-Pail twenty-three kilomètres (or fourteen miles). It is the chief place of the department of Orne. You enter the city through a very long avenue of small trees, forming, I should imagine, from the number of persons coming out of the town, a kind of promenade. On the right there is a very fine mansion, situated in its own grounds. I pass through the Rue de Bretagne, which contains private houses of a large size, and enter a capacious square, where are situated the museum and Palais de Justice, and the towers of the old castle and adjoining buildings forming the prison. Here a band was playing, which had collected together the *élite* of Alençon. I mingled among the crowd, and felt my knapsack to be a kind of letter of introduction; for while it accounted for, at the same time it excused my presence there without being clothed with the garments of fashion. I never saw anywhere else in Normandy so many pretty girls, nor so nicely dressed, as these on society's parade-ground at Alençon. It is only very rarely that the pedestrian traveller encounters such a gathering.

Beyond this square there is a public promenade. The principal street for shops is the Grand Rue, a fine and long street. I visited the cathedral. The exterior is very plain, with a short, ugly tower. The west side, however, is finely worked with small pillars. The interior of the cathedral consists of a nave, with some old painted windows and a choir, and, on the whole, is rather striking. Alençon is a very fine town, with good broad streets; but it wears a very modern appearance. I put up at the Hôtel Grand Cerf, a very large establishment, and extremely well-conducted, clean, and moderate in its charges. There was a goodly assemblage of respectably-dressed gentlemen at the *table d'hôte*, consisting, I think, principally of commercial travellers. One of them I bowed to at the further end of the table I had met somewhere previously. This circumstance led to a running comment on the course of my travels, which, reaching my quarter, was taken up by the next-hand neighbour, who immediately discovered the round-about way I had come from place to place, and that I ought to have taken this and that direction or route. I endeavoured, though unsuccessfully, to convince him that mere progression was not with me an object, but to select such a route as would take me through the most picturesque and interesting parts of the country. This inability on the part of a native to understand and appreciate the feelings of a stranger is very unaccountable. Yet in my own neighbourhood I have occasionally suffered from the same sort of obtuseness, when a passing stranger has remarked, "What a beautiful place!" or, "Is that a church?" when, in fact, it is devoted to very different purposes; or, "How calm and quiet it must be here!" when I feel only too glad to get away. In the evening I went out to an adjoining café.

Monday, Sept. 28th.—It was wet, and I remained at Alençon. Before breakfast I walked in a fine promenade of chesnut trees at the end of the town, on the road to Mortagne. I breakfasted at the Café de la Rotonde, a very fine room; then I walked in the public promenade, which, I presume, from there being a street of that name, is known as the Park, though it scarcely deserves that designation. At the further end there is a nursery-garden, containing a very good collection of dahlias. Then I saw the church of St. Léonard, which is a building worthy of observation, having quite a cathedral-looking interior.

In the course of the day I inspected the cathedral with greater particularity. The nave, with the groined roof and old painted glass windows, is certainly very fine, and improves on a more intimate acquaintance; but the aspect of the church generally is much marred by the modern and plain choir. A closed door prevents your seeing the stone steps leading through the pillar to the pulpit. The exterior of the nave at the west end is very finely worked, but the tower over the choir is ugly. The cathedral, on the north side, is shut in by the adjoining houses, and not thereby seen to advantage.

I visited the Museum, which contains a small collection of coins, fossils, and birds, and a few paintings, one—the scene being apparently the Marriage of Joseph and the Virgin—a subject I never remember seeing treated before. Joseph is in the act of putting a ring on the finger of the Virgin. However, I doubt whether rings in the case of marriage are of so early an origin. The painter's name is Jouinnet, 1691. I read in the "Alençon Journal," that the present museum is not large enough, one collection given to it being excluded from want of space. It is in contemplation to remove the museum to a large house in the Rue de la Marche, having a garden containing part of the old ramparts, and in which there might be annexed buildings if necessary. How strange it seems, that the sojourner in a place for a brief while should take so much interest in any improvements going on there. I remember when at Great Yarmouth some years ago, becoming quite taken and fascinated with the idea of the new pier which, though I believe it has been built, I have never seen, and on which I shall probably never walk.

I observe a fine building containing the public library, open every day, except Sundays and Tuesdays, from twelve to two o'clock; but

I was not there until after the prescribed time, and I did not seek admission as a stranger. Indeed, one public library is so much like another, that to see such a collection apart from the splendour of any building in which it may be deposited, is hardly worth while. Where you have ample time to wander up and down at leisure, and inspect the backs of the books, and here and there take one down, or examine old prints, such a visit may then prove both interesting and instructive. I like also to have a quiet look at the library of a person in whom I feel any curiosity. The kind of books you see there will indicate the course of a man's reading, and will thereby show the furniture of his mind, and be some index to his disposition and character.

The Préfecture is a curious old brick building, and the Tribunal de Commerce is an ancient-looking edifice. Parts of the old ramparts still remain, and there are several very curious antiquated houses in different parts of the town. Alençon is well supplied with hotels and cafés. The café I resorted to this evening is more what one would expect to see in Paris than in a provincial city.

Tuesday, Sept. 29th.—Having settled my bill with the hostess in the bureau in a pleasant manner, for she was a kindly woman, I left Alençon this morning before breakfast. Shortly after quitting the place, a commercial traveller offered me a lift in his *voiture,* which I accepted. He did not, however, proceed more than about two kilomètres (or a mile and a half) in my direction, and having reached a turning to some mills, I descended from the vehicle and parted from my obliging friend. I then walked on to Le Ménil Broux, a village thirteen kilomètres (or eight miles) from Alençon. There is a curious little old church here, with a singular round and large font.

I entered an inn at Le Ménil Broux, and asked the landlady in the kitchen for some breakfast. She was a young, good-looking woman, and apparently a widow, but though doing menial work, she insisted on her dignity in an amusing way. She replied, I must speak to the servant there; so turning to a dirty maid-of-all-work, I repeated my request to that important functionary, and she civilly said she would bring me some breakfast into the *salle à manger.* After waiting some time, I at length perceived some one near me, and on looking up was surprised to see the young mistress herself bringing the things, a very inconsistent line of conduct I thought, after her assertion of dignity in the kitchen; but after all, perhaps, it was only a bit of temper, and possibly on account of my having stumbled the wrong way into the inn. However, I could not afford to take umbrage at any conduct, for it was now about mid-day, and I had not broken my fast this morning. I hoped to find some inn at an earlier stage, but this is the only one hereabouts. Presently three or four jolly countrymen came in, and sat down to a prepared breakfast *à la fourchette;* but I was not asked to join them, as is the hospitable custom at most places, and would have proved most welcome this morning, as my own fare, being pot-luck, was very indifferent. It is a melancholy fact, but nevertheless true, that, as a general rule, a monopoly on the part of an innkeeper leads to inattention, indifference, and sometimes even incivility. Such conduct is the more to be regretted because it necessarily leads travellers who stay at hotels in towns to attribute many acts of real, disinterested kindness to mercenary motives, or the stimulating process of competition, and the consequent existence of rivals. This young widow evidently reigns supreme along the country side, and treats her customers accordingly. But, perhaps, innkeepers in this respect are no worse than their neighbours. It is said that even judges would not always administer justice if it were not for the controlling influence of the press, and that medical men and attorneys would sometimes destroy our lives or estates, were it not from the wholesome check of an action for negligence.

After leaving Le Ménil Broux, the road for some distance proceeds along the outskirts of a forest. I reach Le Mesle-sur-Sarthe, ten kilomètres (or six miles) from Le Ménil Broux. This is a canton town, with a large new church, and some good hotels and cafés. I had a cup of coffee here, and then again started on my journey to Mortagne-sur-Huine, distant sixteen kilomètres (or nine miles) from Le Mesle-sur-Sarthe. I pass on the left a crucifix of iron, on a stone pedestal, erected in the reign of Louis XV. The scenery to-day all the way between Alençon and Mortagne does not present anything particular or striking; but, nevertheless, it is a rural and not unpleasant walk. It is an imperial road between Alençon and Mortagne.

Mortagne is seen on the road for upwards of three miles away, with the church as the most conspicuous object. It is not a town of much pretensions considering its position as chief place of the arrondissement. Mortagne consists of a square, and several pretty good streets. I observed a wretched little square, with a promenade of trees and seats, and having a building, apparently the Palais de Justice, at the bottom, and the prison on the right. I walked through a gateway, apparently part of the old ramparts. Near it, to the left, I saw a curious old arched gateway, leading to what seems to be a private house.

I visited the church, which is a fine edifice, though much shut in by the surrounding houses. The pendants hanging from the nave and choir are worth observing.

I then proceeded to search for the Hôtel de France, mentioned in "Murray's Handbook," but could not find it; indeed, several persons stated that there was not now, and never had been, such a hotel in the town. Accordingly I entered the Hôtel de la Bouille in the square, and asked the landlady for a bed-room; she replied, "Is it only for one night?" Though instinctively conscious that the question meant something to my prejudice, yet on the principle that "honesty is the best policy," I answered in the affirmative. She then lead the way upstairs to a small ill-furnished room, with a creaky tumble-down door; but as it was not unclean, and I was weary, I did not make any demur, but took up my quarters there. I think a traveller might well evade or refuse to answer such a question, as an honest answer invariably leads to some such result as in the present instance.

At the *table d'hôte* there were four persons besides myself—two apparently commercial travellers, a gentleman's coachman, and a boy. I carved the dinner; it was good enough, but wretchedly served, after great delay between the courses, by a waiting-maid. She was rallied about marriage by one of the guests, and in the way of beauty certainly her husband will possess an acquisition; but, unless she mends her ways, not in any other sense. The whole inn here is badly managed, both hostess and maid are hurrying about without any apparent cause, and to the certain neglect of the guests. I asked the girl to mend some socks any time during the evening; she promised to do so. The next morning, after opening the rickety door with difficulty, they were not there. I rang the bell, and on the boots, a boy, appearing, inquired for the socks; presently he brought them carefully folded up, instead of loose as I gave them out, and they were not mended! It was no doubt intended that I should only make the discovery after I had left the inn.

After dinner I strolled out into the town, and took a cup of coffee at a café. I observed the Hôtel de Grand Cerf, in an out-of-the-way street, which has the appearance of being very clean and good. The *salle à manger*, which I saw through the open window, with the *débris* of the *table d'hôte* dinner well attended, looked extremely comfortable. I imagine this must be the best hotel in the place; indeed, the only other apparently, with the exception of that in the square, where I am staying. There is a curious old house used as an inn near the market-place.

Wednesday, Sept. 30th.—Where you meet with incivility or inattention at an inn, I fear reproach, or remonstrance, or what is vulgarly termed "kicking up a row," is of very little service; besides, it disturbs the mind and interferes with the comfort of travelling. But I find that if you can, as they say, touch the pocket, this course, which may be adopted silently, has some effect. Of course, at the regular hotel, where the attendance is down in the bill, there is no mode of effecting such punishment, except, perhaps, on the innocent and unoffending boots; but then at such hotels anything uncivil rarely takes place. It is at country inns where the traveller sometimes meets with positive inattention. Here you may never be again, but if you wish silently to maintain your own dignity, and at the same time to protect the interests of future travellers, withhold any gratuity; simply pay the bill, or amount of the reckoning, and nothing more, and such a step will produce a wonderful effect. This morning certainly I carry out my own precept. The hostess makes out the bill, and gives me a great deal of copper change, as if to invite gratuities. The pretty maid is standing by. I slowly count the money, put the coins in my pocket, make a saluting bow, and quietly depart, leaving both mistress and maid in mute astonishment, and evidently doubting whether my conduct proceeded from ignorance or design.

There is an imperial road between Mortagne and Verneuil, whither I am bound to-day. The distance is thirty-eight kilomètres (or twenty-two miles). The country between the two places is flat, and there is no scenery. I breakfasted at a wayside inn. I passed through St. Maurice, a large village. The church here has a fine spire, and a nave and choir, with a painted and ornamented roof. Soon after leaving St. Maurice, I pass out of the department of Orne and re-enter that of Eure. I observe, further on, a small roadside chapel, dedicated to the Virgin.

It was dark when I reached Verneuil, so that I could see nothing distinctly, and the place is not lit with gas. It consists partly of a long, straggling street, up which I walked for some distance, when seeing no appearance of an inn, I asked an intelligent boy to direct me to the Hôtel de la Poste. He said it was straight on at the entrance of the town in the direction I had come. So I retraced my steps, and observing something like an inn, I opened a door and stepped down among some straw strewed on the floor. At first I thought it was a stable, but a woman at work with her needle at once accosted me with the question, " Have you got a passport?" This I thought certainly very cool, considering that I should have anticipated it would be deemed an honour for me to appear here at all under any circumstances. However, I replied, " Yes; but passports are now abolished in France." The good woman did not require to see it, but showed me at once to a bed-room, and in the course of time furnished a tolerable meal in a small *salle à manger*. " Murray's Handbook" is incorrect in stating that there are two inns here called respectively the Poste and Cheval Blanc. In fact, they form only one hotel, or rather two names for the same hotel.

I presume, from the inquiry made by my hostess, that Verneuil is a place little resorted to by the English tourist. Though passports are no longer required in France, yet this incident shows the expediency of carrying one with you. It serves as a kind of letter of introduction, or guarantee of respectability, and, in many cases, would remove suspicion when other means fail.

CHAPTER X.

Verneuil.—The church of the convent—Nuns at service—Reflections on their mode of life—The church of Notre Dame—St. Laurent—La Tour Grise—A jovial miller—Church of L'Hobital—The Madeleine—St. Jean—Place de la Madeleine—A cracked basin—An unpleasant departure—Breteuil—An unfrequented road—A cunning dog—A poacher—A wild country—The forest of Evreux—Twilight—Reach Evreux—Hotel du Grand Cerf—Full of guests—Bad accommodation—A primitive ball-room—The cathedral—The bishop's garden—The palace—The bishop at prayers—The cloisters—Church of St. Taurin—Public buildings—Picturesque villages—Louviers—A very pretty girl—Hôtel du Mouton.

Thursday, Oct. 1st.—Before breakfast I spent two hours in visiting the churches of Verneuil. First I saw that of the convent, which was undergoing some repairs, and to this accidental circumstance I believe I owed the opportunity of admission. The choir is very elegant, but the other part of the building is plain. The nuns were at service in the body of the church, carefully shut in by a black veil or screen from the vulgar gaze of the workmen. I put aside the veil, and looked on the scene within the church, which was certainly strange, and such as I had never beheld before. There, engaged in prayer, were rows upon rows of young women, evidently of gentle birth, dressed in the sombre garments of the convent—a black gown, with a white collar, and cap as spotless as snow, beneath which a profusion of hair was neatly folded. All looked comely and fair, and there were some faces very pretty, and others with the beauty of advanced womanhood. I was more impressed with the sight of such a general assemblage of fair young nuns than I had ever been by the observation of single instances of individuals in the convent dress one sees in the towns on the Continent.

A disappointment in love, an unhappy home, the forlorn position of the orphan, a constitutional disposition to take a gloomy view of the world, may have led such a one to prefer the religious seclusion of the convent; but what has brought all these here? Surely all, and especially those youthful, bright-looking girls, have not been the victims of ill-starred attachments, or thus early tasted the bitterness of life, or felt the gloom of sorrow. Impossible! Yet, still, why are they here? Religious enthusiasm might explain the reason, had I been present at one of those gorgeous ceremonies of the Roman Catholic ritual which are so calculated to strike the beholder with awe; but nothing could exceed in simplicity this primitive morning service, amid the freshness of the opening day. No Protestant service could be less calculated to excite the mind or rouse the feelings. These girls were simply chanting, with their own sweet voices, some of the prayers of the ordinary daily service, and with method and rhythm, no doubt the result of scientific teaching in the far distant homes from which they have come. No, *this* is not the explanation, and yet I cannot find *the* solution. It may be that, being of the earth, earthy, I cannot understand this spiritual kind of existence.

While wrapt in these thoughts, I became unconscious of all else, and particularly of the fact that I was indulging a forbidden curiosity in thus drawing aside the veil, and seeing this band of virgin worshippers. At least, I was soon reminded of the circumstance by the approach of one of the nuns, probably the superioress, for she looked elderly, though only by comparison with her youthful charges. Though her advance was intended as a rebuke, yet she looked not unkindly. We saluted, I dropped the curtain, and the scene passed away from before the eye, though it still remains engraven on the memory.

As I left the church, and walked back through the grounds, I could not refrain from reflecting whether the life these girls are passing be really useful, or conformable to what may be termed the fitness of things. They have, indeed, forsaken the joys of domestic society; but have they not, also, fled from its duties, trials, and responsibilities? Is not prayer intended to consecrate work, and render man more fit to engage in the active occupations of the world, but not form his only employment? Are you not anticipating the time when work, and labour, and sorrow, and suffering shall be no more, and a time of rest and prayer begin?

I feel, however, somewhat reproved by a sight which immediately presents itself to my view. A young girl, with her bag of books, is tripping lightly towards the convent gates, with a pleased expression of countenance, such as I have never seen displayed in the case of schoolgirls in England, except on those occasions when, in the early summer morning, I have observed them in the vans, in the streets of London, on their way to the annual feast in the country. "So," thought I, "these fair nuns do not spend all their time in prayer and meditation. I did them an injustice there. They keep a school, and treat their scholars so well, and teach them so kindly, that it becomes a pleasure to attend there." Though withdrawn from the world themselves, they are willing to impart to young girls that knowledge which will enable them to succeed in some practical calling, and combined with the higher teaching, without which secular learning will only tend to bitterness and sorrow.

Then I went to the Church of Notre Dame. This, though very small, is quite a miniature cathedral, and by far the most magnificent little church I have seen in Normandy. It is quite a gem. The exterior, however, is much spoiled in appearance by the ungainly spire, being of that extinguisher shape so common among the small town and village churches. It contains a nave, transept, and choir. The nave has short, thick pillars, finely worked above. The *tout ensemble* of this church is truly beautiful. There are fine painted glass windows, which altogether present a most gorgeous appearance. Many of them are of saints. There is one window devoted to a history of the Virgin. In the first compartment she is presented as a little girl by her mother in the Temple. Then are depicted the angel appearing to announce the immaculate conception, the birth of our Saviour, the presentation of the infant Jesus in the Temple, the Saviour appearing on some occasion to the Virgin, her death, and ascension into heaven.

The Church of St. Laurent is now in decay, and used as a carpenter's shop. I inspected La Tour Grise, a very large building, part of the old fortifications. A flour mill is romantically situated near here. The miller, a fat, jovial-looking man, seeing a stranger, came out from his domain, and, having accosted me, entered into some explanation as to the origin and history of the town, which I did not note down, as probably it would be somewhat wide of the mark, as is generally the case with local information.

I noticed the old church of L'Hobital, now fallen into disuse, and turned into a warehouse. Afterwards, I saw the Madeleine, the principal church in Verneuil. The tower is certainly a fine specimen of architecture, and it is a conspicuous object for miles round. The interior of the church is large, but exceedingly plain. I then walked on and observed the church of St. Jean, which has a fine tower, but it is now in decay, and used as a warehouse for grain.

The Place de la Madeleine is a fine square. There is a hotel near here called the Hôtel du Grand St. Martin, which, from outward appearance, I should imagine is the best in the place. On the outskirts of the town there are some fine boulevards or promenades.

After making the tour of the town, I returned to the Hôtel de la Poste. I did not leave the inn without some unpleasantness. I had a cracked basin in my room, which I no sooner put my foot into than it broke in pieces. I called attention to the circumstance at the time, the evening of my arrival, and it was at once replaced by another, without my version of the matter being disputed, but this morning, in the bill, I find I am charged full price for the old piece of crockery, I forget how many francs. To this charge I demur, but in vain, then at least for some reduction, but with the same result. The idea that I should wash my feet at all, seemed to the landlady quite ludicrous, and in a basin, too; she had never heard of such a thing; no wonder that it was broken. Everything, also, down to the bread, item by item, was charged, which, though it may amount to about the same thing, is a custom I much abhor. However, there seemed nothing to be done but to pay the bill. I certainly resorted to my practice on these occasions, and withheld any gratuity to the servant girl, as she stoutly took the side of her mistress, but apparently without effect, for neither seemed to notice any omission on my part; but the bone of contention being removed, both appeared inclined to civility had I permitted such a demonstration in my favour. But my temper was ruffled, so in anger I departed.

I experienced some little difficulty on the confines of the town, in finding the direction I required, but at last I am on the departmental road to Breteuil. The country is very flat and without scenery. Shortly before entering Breteuil, there is a fine avenue of poplar trees. Breteuil is a canton town, increasing in importance, and containing many new houses and a fine public building in the course of erection. It has a good hotel apparently, and many excellent cafés. The church is a large but plain building. There is, however, to the right as you enter the place, a curious old ornamented Lady Chapel, which, to judge from the painted glass windows, the figures on which are very quaint, must be extremely ancient.

After leaving Breteuil, I took the turning to the right, along a road of grand communication, which leads to Evreux. The road is little frequented, indeed, I hardly met a soul all the way, but on that very account, there being scarcely any traffic, it is soft and pleasant walking for the feet. The country around is desolate and unenclosed. I am amused at the action of a dog, which is sitting on a bank by the wayside. On seeing my approach it retreats along the field to the rear, but when I pass, and am discovered to be nothing dangerous, the animal comes back slowly, as if returning from a constitutional, and impelled by no sense of fear, and resumes his exact former position with great dignity. It is not often you see a dog show any sign of fear, and I always pity the occurrence. My sympathies are, therefore, with the poor animal on this occasion. No doubt, the unwonted sight along this unfrequented road of a man walking with a knapsack, put the animal off its guard. Presently I see a fine tortoiseshell-looking dog coming stealthily along the edge of the turf on the roadside the furthest from me, with head skulking and tail down; but he evidently is suffering from the effects of that evil conscience which makes cowards of us all, for this animal, if I mistake not, coming as he did from the direction of a small covert, has been poaching.

The country is barren and wild, and the reader will readily believe my assertion when I state that, to while away the time, I took to the composition of an imaginary sermon, that last resource of the unemployed mind. Presently I enter the forest of Evreux, through the heart of which the road wends its solitary way. There is, however, some variety here—trees, brushwood, long grass, and wild flowers; these enliven the eye of a traveller through a wood, and prove refreshing to his senses. Though there is some danger, perhaps, here, as I contemplate that wolves have not altogether disappeared from the forests of Normandy.

After emerging from the forest, twilight came on, and ere I reached Evreux it was quite dark. I entered the city along a road by the river's bank, as I discovered next day, unprotected, and into which I might easily have stepped, for on this night there was no moon to disclose, by its friendly rays, the track for the benighted traveller. On reaching Evreux, I had to inquire a good deal—to walk here, there, and about before I could discover the Hôtel du Grand Cerf, which was at the furthest end of the town. Arrived there, I found a good deal of bustle and animation; the hotel was evidently full of guests. I was accommodated with a bed-room, small, and at the top of the house; no tooth-glass, nor could I obtain one; and, moreover, I was disturbed with a flea in the night, almost the only insect of that or any other kind I encountered in Normandy. This hotel may be first-rate, but it did not prove so to me. The *table d'hôte* was long over, but I came in for the remains of the repast, which, with a bottle of *vin ordinaire*, turned out reasonably satisfactory. I may observe that the distance between Verneuil and Evreux is forty kilomètres (or twenty-four miles).

On going to my room, and looking out of the window, a strange scene presented itself. There was in appearance a ball-room of considerable size, full of persons in evening dress dancing to the playing of a piano. I could see the dancers bounding down the room in my direction, and again turning and disappearing from view. The waltz and galop seemed the principal dances. I thought at first it must be some casino in the precincts, but on observation I noticed several very young girls, quite children, among the dancers; and thus such a supposition did not seem probable, for they at least, whoever and whatever their relatives, would not be subjected to such a scene of temptation. So I gave up the solution of the matter, and retired to rest; but next morning I was curious enough to go out into the yard of the hotel on a voyage of discovery, and there to the right I found a very small, rough, extempore ball-room, with a diminutive piano. This was the simple solution of the matter; the guests in the hotel had been dancing there, but the room was so very small that it seemed perplexing how any movements of even a few people could take place there; and yet this little chamber had in the darkness become magnified into a splendid saloon, so deceptive is the sight when the guidance of light is removed from the scene. A gentleman at the breakfast-table asked me if I had joined in the dance of the evening before, so I presume such entertainments are customary here, and would, no doubt, prove an agreeable diversion to travellers who should remain at this hotel two or three days, long enough to form some acquaintanceship with the young French ladies, and thus, in a rough and ready kind of way, see a little of provincial society. I presume, from the remarks this gentleman makes, that the dancers kept it up till late at night, though, being fatigued with much walking, their noise did not prevent me soon falling asleep.

Friday, Oct. 2nd.—Evreux is the chief place of the department of Eure. Before breakfast I spent an hour in looking over the cathedral. The exterior is very striking, but much marred by the spires of two of the towers being apparently added through the original ones not having been completed. The interior of the cathedral is, on the whole, very grand and magnificent. The rose window in the south transept is particularly beautiful. The Lady Chapel, with its painted glass windows, and the woodwork enclosing the chapels around the choir, are worthy of observation. The general view from the west end of the cathedral, of the nave and choir, is rather contracted, owing to the arches being too narrow. I walked into the bishop's garden, the gateway being left open, though I fear that I was a trespasser there, from the horror an elderly female displayed on coming out of some building and seeing me there. On my departure she immediately shut the gates, to prevent any similar intrusion within these sacred premises. There were some nice retired walks, and a very good kitchen garden, altogether giving one an idea of great seclusion and comfort. The palace is a fine-looking building, with a communication by a covered way connecting it with the cathedral. When I first entered the cathedral in the morning the bishop was at prayers in one of the small chapels, and at their conclusion he was escorted back through the private entrance with great solemnity. I visited the cloisters; there is here a curious old piece of tapestry.

After breakfast I walked about the city again. I inspected the church of St. Taurin, the general effect of which is good. The Hôtel de Ville, the Cours d'Assizes, and the Beffroi, or Tour de l'Horloge, are public buildings worth noticing. There are many old timber-built houses about the streets, and altogether Evreux is a city ancient in appearance, and extremely interesting to visit.

To-day I walked from Evreux to Louviers, twenty-two kilomètres (or thirteen miles), along the imperial road. There is no scenery, but shortly before reaching Louviers the view of one or two villages nestling beneath the hills to the right is very picturesque. Louviers is the chief place of the arrondissement, and, to judge from the mills I pass, a town of some manufacturing importance.

On entering the place, I observed the prettiest girl I had seen in Normandy. She was engaged with some women washing linen on a barge on the river, near the bridge. She was working as hard as any of them, and yet showed no symptoms of fatigue. The act of washing, so far from being ungainly, showed her lithe figure to great advantage. Her hair was nicely arranged, and she was dressed with great neatness. There was composure in this young girl's manner, and grace in her every attitude. Her face was a perfect model of beauty, and nothing could exceed the delicate and finely-formed proportions of her frame. I stand on the bridge enthralled, and with a gaze too fixed, I fear, for soon I attract the girl's attention, and am obliged to feign some other object of view. But why is this fair and lovely girl here? Is there no fairy prince to come and take her away to his distant palace, where, her humble parentage being unknown, her beauty may reign supreme?

After such a rhapsody, I owe almost an apology to the reader for recording the prosaic fact, that on reaching Louviers I took up my quarters at the Hôtel du Mouton.

CHAPTER XI.

Louviers—Church of Notre Dame—Maison des Templiers—Out of Eure into Seine Inférieure—Caudebec—Elbeuf—The churches of St. Jean and St. Etienne—Orival; the chapel there—A route little traversed—A cart without springs—Grand Couron—A friendly Frenchman—An unromantic word—A dark walk—A lost cat—The suburbs of Rouen—Suggested route through the forest—Rouen—Politeness at a café—The Hôtel d'Angleterre—The cathedral—Church of St. Maclou—St. Ouen—Public gardens—Library—Gallery of paintings—Museum—Palais de Justice—Other public buildings—Church of St. Vincent—General description of Rouen—An earthquake on the spot—An excellent hotel.

Saturday, Oct. 3rd.—Early this morning I visited the church of Notre Dame at Louviers. It is a fine edifice. The south portal is particularly striking. I observed the painted glass windows and the filigree work in the southern part of the central tower. According to "Murray's Handbook," there are some bas-reliefs containing subjects from Scripture, but I could not find them. Louviers is a large town, and resounds with mills. There is an old wooden house newly done up, called the ancient house of St. Martin, which was probably the Maison des Templiers.

I walked this morning from Louviers to Elbeuf, sixteen kilomètres (or nine miles). You proceed along the imperial road for a short distance, and then turn to the left. It is a departmental road, barren, and without scenery. Elbeuf is approached through a townlike looking suburb, called Caudebec, shortly before reaching which I pass out of the department of Eure and re-enter that of Seine Inférieure. Elbeuf is a good-sized, straggling canton town. I observed two or three hotels, but none good. I had some breakfast *à la fourchette* at a tolerable restaurant.

After breakfast I visited the churches at Elbeuf. That of St. Jean has a very fine tower — the most conspicuous object in the town—and some fine glass windows. The church consists of a nave simply; the choir being merely a part of it divided by some rails. The general effect is fine. The church of St. Etienne has a stunted spire, but the interior is on the same plan as the church of St. Jean. The painted window presented by the clothworkers is in the church of St. Etienne, and not in that of St. Jean, as incorrectly stated in "Murray's Handbook." I saw a small church to the right, apparently in a suburb.

After leaving Elbeuf I walked to Orival. Here the rocks of that name begin. I visited the chapel, most picturesquely situated on the ledge of the rocks. It has a small churchyard. From this spot a fine view is obtained of Elbeuf, the Seine, and the rocks. The exterior of the church or chapel is much spoilt by an ugly stunted spire, perched on a ledge of the rock, without being actually joined to the building, apparently a modern addition. There is also added an ugly brick structure for a vestry or sacristy. In other respects the exterior of the church is fine. But the inside presents the very beau idéal of a village church. It consists of a nave and two side aisles, finely arched, with hanging pendants. The chapel contains oak pews, and the pulpit is near the centre. The part forming the choir is paved with coloured marble. There are some painted windows, one of them representing Moses staying the plague, with a dog by his side.

The road from Orival proceeds in a valley between two hills, which shut out the view of the Seine. I presume the route along here is little traversed by tourists. A woman expressed some surprise at my walking, and a countryman induced me to enter his cart, but unfortunately it had no springs, and as the driver apparently put on extra speed on my account, I was jolted and shaken in the most merciless manner. It was far worse than walking would be to the most fatigued traveller. I think, in order to appreciate that great modern invention of springs to vehicles, we ought to drive a short distance in a country cart like the present. We should thus, also, be able to realize the discomforts of locomotion which must have been experienced by our ancestors; and perhaps such a reason may have induced them to refrain from increasing the speed of their conveyances, when they could only do so at the risk of so much personal inconvenience. Fortunately, my friend, at the end of about two kilomètres (or a mile and a half), stopped, and said he went no further. I got down and thanked him, though I was much surprised at the destination, as we were merely on the borders of a large field, without a house near, or a side road, or lane, or turning of any kind. Being curious to know where my friend was going, I presently looked back, and saw him drive the cart over the bank, and then along the field at a brisk pace towards a house in the distance.

I walked on and soon reached Grand Couron, an inferior canton town. Here there is a small inn, which the countryman, indeed, strongly recommended; but it did not look very inviting, and therefore, though twilight was approaching, I determined to push on for Rouen to-night. The church at Grand Couron contains a choir, consisting of a part of the building separated by an archway, very much in the same manner as the chancel of an English church.

The road between Louviers and Grand Couron is departmental; but at the latter place I fall into the imperial road to Rouen. Shortly after passing Grand Couron, and on ascending a hill, I fell into conversation with a Frenchman driving a *voiture* containing himself and wife. He was walking just now, to rest the horse. He soon found out my country, and then spoke English very well, at which I expressed some surprise, and asked whether he had been living in England. He replied, "Yes, in London, for several years;" and thus we suddenly became fast friends. He apologized for not giving me a lift, as the *voiture* would not contain three. Moreover, Madame was stout; therefore his excuse was quite sincere. My friend says that there is a shorter way to Rouen by about three kilomètres (or two miles), through the forest. You turn off at the foot of this hill to the right, about four kilomètres (or two and a half miles) from Grand Couron. He is pointing the road below there with his whip, and saying, sympathetically, that I shall meet with no 'Bus along the road to Rouen. I feel half inclined to follow his advice and turn back, when there comes driving up the hill a *voiture* containing two men, one of them being a woodman of the forest. On being appealed to by my friend, he does not quite indorse his statement as to the way being so much shorter; moreover, he says that the road is bad and lonely. So I determine to pursue my course. The loneliness, indeed, I do not dread, for by this time I have acquired thorough confidence in the Norman character; but to make one's way in the dark, along a road full of ruts, is by no means easy, and renders practically longer the shorter way.

The *voitures*, having reached the summit of the hill, drove on, and I was alone. There was something very unromantic in that short word 'Bus. It seemed all at once to transport me back to London, its busy streets and ceaseless hum. But now the night fell, and there was no moon, and travelling became lonely and weirdlike, and darkness brooded over the face of the landscape. Presently my friend, who had stopped somewhere, passed me at full speed, with a genial English " good night," which rang through the silent air. Then I met no human soul; but as I passed on there came up to me from the side of the road a poor cat, mewing piteously, as if entreating one to lead her home, for she has evidently wandered far away and lost herself. On these occasions we realize the great gulf which separates us from the dumb animals. They can only explain their wants in an undefined sort of way—we often can make no intelligible reply. If so, I should like to explain to the poor cat that I am an utter stranger, coming along this road for the first time, and unable therefore to direct her homeward. As it is, I walk on in silence, and still hear behind me the piteous wail of the poor animal, which is rendered the more clear from the stillness of the scene around.

At length I reach the suburbs of Rouen, and the region of street lamps. But the way still seemed long before arriving at any civilized part of the city. Not that the distance come to-day is very great, but I had been occupied some time at the places *en route*. It is twenty-two kilomètres (or thirteen miles) between Elbeuf and Rouen, making in all, from Louviers to this city, thirty-eight kilomètres (or twenty-two miles). There is no scenery between Orival and Rouen; therefore, the pedestrian who reaches the forest earlier in the day would, I think, act wisely by taking that route, which, no doubt, he would find more pleasant than the imperial road.

I stopped at a café when I reached the centre of Rouen. On rising to depart, I was quite overwhelmed with the politeness of the waiters, two of whom rushed forward to adjust my knapsack. Then I passed through several of the principal streets, and across the bridge over the Seine, where I paid an infinitesimal sum—I forget exactly how little. Here, on the Quay, I found the object of my search, the Hôtel d'Angleterre, which I reached about eleven o'clock. The landlord received me at the entrance with quiet courtesy, and called an elegantly dressed and handsome chambermaid. She showed me to a very good bedroom, which formed an appropriate termination to a day of much fatigue.

Sunday, Oct. 4th.—I breakfasted at a café, and then proceeded to visit the cathedral. I ascended one of the towers, from which a good view of the whole city is obtained. The church of St. Ouen is particularly striking. You also have a good view of the church of St. Maclou, and see the small church of St. Gervais in the distance. A bird's-eye view like the present gives the stranger, at the expense of little time and trouble, an excellent idea of a place, even though it be a large city. The exterior of the cathedral is very fine, with the exception of the modern spire of one of the towers, which is very ugly. I observed the arches in the nave, the Grecian screen, the woodwork in the choir, the screen and door of the sacristy, and the lady chapel, containing the monuments, and the end chapel. There are two rose windows, one in the west, and the other in the north transept. The window in the south transept is quite plain.

Then I visited the church of St. Maclou, observing the woodwork of the portals. It is a fine church, though small. Afterwards I proceeded to the church of St. Ouen. This edifice is certainly grand and magnificent, but it more struck me as a whole than from any particular details. There is an appearance of completeness and immensity about the church calculated to impress the beholder. I observed the slab over the tomb of the architect of the church, in the chapel of St. Agnes. Most particularly I remarked the rose windows in the north and south transept, but could not discover the striking superiority of the north over that of the south, which, according to the story of rivalry, so exasperated the builder.

I visited the public gardens, which are pretty good. A band was playing. Then I had a glance at the public library, though I was obliged to retire, as it was not open to the public. I went over the gallery of paintings. There are two pictures more deserving of notice than the others, that of " Trajan and the Widow," and the one of the " Virgin and Child among Saints and Angels."

Then I proceeded to the Museum of Antiquities. I saw the painted glass windows, the charters, including that signed by William the Conqueror by a cross, the small Gothic kind of chapel which contained the relics of Saint Sever, and the glass case said to contain the remains of the heart of Richard Cœur de Lion, and other curiosities.

Then I saw over the Palais de Justice, a very magnificent building. I was shown over the Civil Court, the Court of Tribunal of the First Instance, the Court of Appeal and the Criminal Court, and a noble introductory kind of hall, answering the same purpose as Westminster Hall. Then, under the guidance of a young man from the concierge at the Palais de Justice, I saw the Tour de la Grosse Horloge, the Place de la Pucelle d'Orleans, where Joan of Arc was burnt, with the statue in the centre, and the Hôtel du Bourgtheroude. Afterwards I walked into the church of St. Vincent, and observed the fine painted glass windows there.

Rouen is the old capital of Normandy. At present it occupies the position of chief place of the department of Seine Inférieure. It is a magnificent city, with fine streets and quays. The Rue Imperiale is a good street, and the Place de la Hôtel de Ville a fine square. The Rue Grand Pont, and the streets in extension of it, are also greatly to be admired, and the Suspension Bridge over the Seine looks well.

I read afterwards that on this Sunday there was the shock of an earthquake felt at Rouen, but I neither experienced, nor heard, nor perceived anything unusual. The city was perfectly calm and quiet, and the forces of nature seemed hushed amid the calmest composure.

Having thus spent the day in seeing the lions of Rouen, I returned to the Hôtel d'Angleterre, and was able to appreciate the liberal fare placed before us by our worthy host at the *table d'hôte*. This was well attended and excellently served. This hotel is one of the best and most comfortable I have stayed at during my travels in Normandy. It is scrupulously clean, and the landlord is most attentive. There is a small salon for sitting and reading. You can step out at once on a fine quay, which forms a good promenade, or you may lounge on the Suspension Bridge, and look down on the gently-flowing Seine.

CHAPTER XII.

Reasons for detaining the attention of the reader—Nature of the scenery—Climate—Church architecture—Closing the country churches—Desecration of old churches—Middle-class worshippers—Absence of wayside crosses—Public gardens—Modes of travelling—Passports—French money—The country inns—Cider—Vin ordinaire—Melons—Tripe—Cleanliness of the beds—Expense of living—Company at the inns—Mode of salutation—Cafés—Absence of drunkenness—Manners of the Normans—The gentry—Their houses—Flax-spinning—Playing at bowls—Expressions of the peasantry—Personal appearance of the Normans—Beauty of the women—Their bad taste in dress.

BEFORE I ask the reader to accompany me on the remaining short stages of my journey homewards, I would detain his attention in the present chapter while I bring before him the thoughts and reflections I have formed on the country of Normandy, and the habits, manners, and customs of the people. No doubt some of my remarks would be found equally applicable to the rest of France, and perhaps the Continent generally; but I think a traveller stands a better chance of informing or instructing his readers, if he confine himself to his own practical experiences, without reference to the consideration whether they are local or general, common-place or extraordinary.

Normandy is a country of landscapes. The scenery is neither grand nor striking. The mountain towering to the sky is not there, neither the foaming waterfall, nor rocks, nor large trees. Nevertheless there is a quiet beauty about the face of the country which is pleasant to see, though in what, in particular, the eye finds delight, it would be difficult to describe in words. The sensations are not roused by ice and snow, by avalanches, yawning abysses, or dangerous precipices. Here calm and quiet reign supreme, and Nature presents an aspect of peace. One great drawback to the landscape is the absence of water. The rivers are few, and flow in slender streams, and of lakes there are none. Suppose the view from Richmond Hill without the River Thames winding through the valley beneath—what a difference there would be! Or, again, have you never stood on Box Hill, and, while surveying the splendid scene, regretted that no lake or river should be there to lend a charm to the varied landscape? But, notwithstanding these disadvantages, most persons, I believe, will find in Norman scenery much to admire and appreciate, and something also to enchant.

The climate of Normandy is moist, and, therefore, not very invigorating. A great deal of rain falls, scarcely a day passing without some wet. But I found that, during the night, the rain-fall was much greater, frequently coming down in torrents. The effects of rain, however, would soon pass away. Most travellers in Switzerland must remember, unless they were peculiarly favoured with the weather, that, when the rain was over, there still remained clouds enveloping the mountains, and rendering the distant views quite obscure; and that this state of things will sometimes continue for two or three days—thus marring very much the enjoyment of the flying tourist. Not so, however, in Normandy. No sooner has the shower ceased, than the sunshine will break out, and the whole landscape will appear before the eye, only rendered the more charming by the crystal particles on the trees, and the idea of refreshment occasioned by the wet. I have seen a woman rush out of her house to remove clothes from the lines in the presence of a drenching shower, and before she had well reached her door with the basket, the rain had ceased and the sun was shining; so suddenly do the storms come and go. The pedestrian traveller particularly should be warned not to remain in a town of a morning because it is raining there. I have frequently left a town in the wet, and on ascending the hill, and reaching the tableland above, have found it quite dry, and the sun shining; while, on looking back, I have seen the place enveloped in clouds and rain. Of course, the contrary will also be the case; and you may leave the town in the dry, and walk into the wet; or, again, on level land, you may, in the course of a few miles, walk through the rain or dry, as the case may be, and reach the contrary. Therefore, as a general rule, the pedestrian should, like King Ahab, rise up and proceed on his journey, and not let the rain prevent him. There is one exception, perhaps, where the rain is coming down steadily, and the sky is dark and overcast, without clouds here and there, or any interval of blue sky; then, as a rule, it will be found that the rain is general, and not local. The moisture of the climate affords one great advantage to the pedestrian in that it makes the roads soft, and preserves them free from dust. This is an inestimable comfort, and, moreover, conducive to cleanliness.

The principal attraction of Normandy is the church architecture. The cathedrals and principal churches I have attempted feebly to describe, as I have reached them in the course of my travels. There remains something to be said about the small town and village churches scattered up and down throughout the country. These do not bear out the remarks made by travellers as to their being very fine. Those I have been in are very plain and simple—indeed, much more so than the like of a similar kind in Brittany or England. The spires are short and stunted, presenting somewhat of the extinguisher shape, and roofed with rough tiles. I entered many of these churches, until I found one interior so much like another that I became tired of the monotony. I observed, however, in the distance, two or three village churches with fine spires. Still, unquestionably, in this matter, a good deal of exaggeration has prevailed, which, in order to prevent disappointment, it is as well to point out.

The practice prevails in Normandy of closing the country churches, and often shutting the gates of the churchyard, or rather locking them. The unpleasant custom in such respect which exists in England may therefore be attributable to this Norman source. A more objectionable idea, however, is the desecration of old churches, which is calculated to startle the traveller, and offend his religious notions, though he belong to a different faith. Why not have them pulled down and removed, and other buildings more commodious and suitable for the purposes intended erected in their stead? The old materials might be used again, if need be. I mean nothing superstitious. I have referred, when there, to the decayed churches at Caen and Verneuil. On the way between Alençon and Mortagne, I entered a small church, dismantled, and used apparently as a storehouse, though it contained nothing at present. A great part of the high altar still remains unremoved. Such a systematic desecration of disused churches is very extraordinary among a people where the outward ceremonies of religion at least are observed with decorum.

Another circumstance which strikes the traveller in Normandy very forcibly, is the small number of middle-class worshippers among the men in the congregations. Where are they? Do they simply tolerate the religion of the country, without any belief in its efficacy? Or do they send their women to the churches to offer up prayers for them? Certainly, the practical result looks strange and anomalous. One instance, indeed, came under my notice of such a worshipper. It was on a week-day. I was walking about a church, the name of which and the place where I forget. There, in the early morning, in one of the side chapels, was a gentleman dressed in deep mourning. He was in the prime of life, pale, but handsome, and on his countenance were impressed the marks of deep sorrow. He was no publican who smote his hands on his breast, and said only, "God be merciful to me a sinner;" neither was he a Pharisee, for he was engaged in sincere, heartfelt prayer, at a time when no relative, friend, or acquaintance would be likely to be near. I pass on in silent reverence at such a scene, and speculate what can be the cause of such great sorrow. Is it the loss of father, mother, wife, or child, and is he praying for strength under his affliction, or for the repose of the departed soul? The sight was certainly impressive, and one not likely to be soon forgotten.

The traveller who proceeds from Brittany to Normandy will be struck, in the latter country, by the absence of wayside crosses and small buildings dedicated to the Virgin. They hardly exist in Normandy as part of the worship of the country.

The public gardens in Normandy are worthy of notice. These exist in all the large towns, and form one of the institutions of the place. The plan of laying them out is excellent. It consists mainly in making the most of the allotted space. The view of the buildings and country beyond, except in those cases where a good prospect is attainable, is shut out by trees and evergreens, thus giving an idea of space which the actual quantity of the ground would not otherwise convey. Those of my readers who remember and visited the Coliseum at Regent's Park, will recollect what admirable use was made of a very small piece of ground by means of such device. You were surrounded by trees and evergreens, grotto-work, and waterfalls, and singing birds, and rustic walks and seats; but you saw nothing beyond; and without such a special and particular survey as ordinary visitors would not think of making, the size or extent of the premises could not be ascertained. With reference to the enclosures of ground in the squares of London and our large cities and towns, the introduction of a little Norman art in horticulture would effect wonders. The primary mistake here is the making of a broad gravel walk round the enclosure, the primitive idea, I presume, being to permit as long a walk as practicable for the use of those who have the *entrée* of the enclosure. Now, this part should be planted with trees and shrubs, especially evergreens, so as to shut out the gaze of the vulgar, and at the same time convey to the mind of the promenader inside an idea of indefinite space. It may be said, "Why shut out the view, when you are doing nothing to be ashamed of?" The answer is, that the very institution of a garden implies privacy. Does not the want of this mar the enjoyment of the morning walk in the bit of garden attached to a house in the suburbs? Is not the great grievance there that you are overlooked by your neighbours?

Another mistake about the English public garden is, that it frequently, as in the case of Belgrave Square, has a raised ground or eminence in the centre, thus even inviting publicity. Still another error is the intersection in every direction of beds of flowers and plants. No doubt, where the space is very small, this is the best use to turn it to; but where you have a large enclosure of ground, there should be a broad expanse of turf on which to walk and lounge. A public garden should combine as much as possible the qualities of the park and flower-garden. Perhaps the best specimen of a public garden in London, on the principle that "bad is the best," will be found to be the garden of Lincoln's Inn Fields.

The love of a garden implies some degree of civilization. To the uncultivated mind there is great monotony there; always the same trees and shrubs, day by day, week by week, month by month, year by year, and not much variety in the flowers. But the lover of nature sees through a different glass, or the other side of the shield. To him there are great contrasts and changes as the seasons come round. In the early spring the buds attract his attention; the violets, snowdrops, and primroses; then the gradual advance towards the full bloom and foliage of summer forms a constant source of wonder and interest; then for a while there comes the fruition of the year—trees towering and luxuriant with leaves, flowers with their many colours, and soft, velvety turf; then, again, there is the gradual approach towards autumn—the discolouration and decay of the leaves, and their fall, and the withering of flowers and plants; and, last of all, even the depth of winter does not take away from a garden all its attractions, but when the trees and shrubs are covered with snow, or the cold wind echoes through the branches, there is pleasure in the contrast, and in the weird and lifeless aspect which the face of nature presents. Therefore, I think the existence of public gardens in Normandy is a sign of a high degree of civilization. They are kept in good order, and are much appreciated.

With regard to modes of travelling in Normandy, the railways will now be found to lead to all the principal places, and diligences or public *voitures* run where there are no railroads. But the tourist who does not propose walking, would act wisely by driving through the country in a *voiture*. These are very convenient, light, holding only two, with a good horse, and, I believe, not expensive. The better plan would be, where there are two friends, or husband and wife, to hire the *voiture* for a short course through the country, returning to the same place by a different route. Of course, under such circumstances, the driver must be dispensed with, as in the lighter two-wheel vehicle there is no room for him. However, there is a one-horse, four-wheel *voiture*, holding two inside and two out, including the driver. But the beau ideal of driving through the country would be in the light two-wheeler. This has a back, to raise up in case of wet, which effectually protects without incommoding the driver.

As is well known, passports are not now necessary in any part of the French dominions. I am not so sure, however, whether the local regulations as to obtaining the names, and addresses and occupations, of the visitors at hotels, and especially country inns, be not in force still, more or less. These regulations affect Frenchmen as well as foreigners, and are not therefore necessarily abolished with the passport system. I should, therefore, recommend that a passport should be carried still. On these and similar occasions it would be found useful, as also at museums and other public institutions, where a form of introduction is desirable. As I may be addressing some who have not yet travelled on the Continent, I would remark that a Foreign Office passport is procurable on the introduction of any banker, clergyman, barrister, or solicitor, through any tourist shop or office.

For the information also of these readers, I would make a few remarks on French money. The decimal system prevails. The gold coins are, a Napoleon, equal to sixteen shillings, and half and quarter Napoleons. The silver pieces are, a franc, equal to about ninepence, and two-franc, half, and quarter franc coins. There is a five-franc silver piece; but it is becoming scarce, the gold coin of the same amount being found much more convenient and portable. The copper coins are, a two-sous piece, equal to about a penny, and a one-sou piece, and centimes, a very small coin, thin, and of size less than a farthing. Ten centimes go to a two-sous piece, and a hundred centimes, or twenty sous, to a franc; hence the meaning of the decimal system. The centime, like our farthing, is rarely actually seen; though, unlike the lowest coin with us, it is often talked about, and figures a good deal in accounts. But the traveller may proceed through France without once having this little modest coin in his possession. The most likely occasion will be at a bridge, where the gate-keeper will demand two centimes for the right to pass. On handing him a sou he will give in change three centimes, which you will probably be somewhat perplexed to know what to do with. They are too small in amount even to give to a beggar with any charity. I remember, on my first visit to Paris, in 1855, having somehow possession of a centime, which on the return journey to Dieppe I gave, in anger, to a boy who insisted on following me, to carry a small carpet bag; but the poor little fellow, though much surprised, took the matter in such good part, and so courteously, that I regretted the act, though it did not seem to call for any specific reward. Probably, too, he thought that, as a stranger, I was ignorant of the value of the coin.

Still, though the decimal system prevails in France, it is not always adhered to in the process of reckoning in practice. For instance, at a café, instead of the waiter saying forty centimes for your cup of coffee, he will say eight sous. I have found this little matter sometimes perplexing, and therefore I advert to it. I think most of the waiters and shopkeepers at places where tourists resort have learnt this much about our coinage, that a sou is about equal to a halfpenny; and therefore they imagine a mode of counting by sous or halfpence will be more easy to the Englishman than by centimes, anything like the equivalent to which does not exist in our monetary system. But to the Englishman who has endeavoured to master the French decimal system, and to leave his own behind, such a method of reckoning becomes perplexing. However, in the course of a week or so the French money will be found more easy in the reckoning, so simple is their system, than the cumbrous method to which we have been accustomed all our lives.

The traveller in Normandy will at first sight be much disconcerted by the outward appearance of the country inns, which are dirty-looking in aspect, rough in exterior form, and with a kind of stable-yard often in front of them. They are also deficient in one kind of accommodation, which has been observed upon by almost every writer of travels or guide-books relating to France, and the exact nature of which inconvenience will no doubt be readily understood by the reader, from the difficulty felt in stating it in so many words.

But on a nearer approach, and a more intimate acquaintance, the inns will be found to provide and contain all the essentials to the comfort of living, if not also some of the luxuries of life. A *table d'hôte* dinner is served daily, consisting of good soup, fresh fish, and a variety of excellent courses of French dishes. There is sometimes also a *table d'hôte* breakfast at ten o'clock, comprising a meal without soup, and altogether lighter than that of the dinner. The common drink of the country is cider, and this always appears on the table *ad libitum* without charge. The cider varies in quality very much; sometimes extremely good, and at other times so bad that it is difficult to form an idea of the kind of apples or process of making which could produce such a liquor. Acid as vinegar, and more unpalatable than mineral water. I found at the smaller inns, where alone the very worst cider is met with, great honesty in advice on the subject. The waiting-maid, or master, or mistress, would not scruple to condemn the cider when asked as to its quality, if it really deserved condemnation. I always trusted to them in this respect, and therefore, after two or three early experiences, I escaped drinking any very bad cider. Some people, I am aware, do not like this beverage, however good, and under any circumstances. I am very fond of cider, and I found it a particularly refreshing drink after the intense thirst caused by walking. I drank it like a fish, without stint or limit, and never found that it produced any intoxicating effect. However, those travelling in the ordinary way would act wisely in being much more abstemious.

The *vin ordinaire* produced at the Norman inns is pretty good, and of about the same quality as that to be met with at the two-franc restaurants at the Palais Royal at Paris.

Melons abound in Normandy; they grow in beds in the corners of fields, or any odd bit of ground which cannot conveniently be turned to any other use. They appear in profusion, and very ripe and good, and cut up in slices, at the *tables d'hôte*, and served with white sugar. Not only does the table look well with them there, but such fruit as a course, and not in the way of dessert, proves very refreshing to the palate, especially at breakfast. At the country inns tripe is a favourite dish with the Normans. It is cut into very small pieces, and fried.

There is one matter appertaining to the inns in Normandy which is most especially worthy of notice; that is, the cleanliness of the beds. The linen may be coarse, and sometimes of the roughest material imaginable; and the floor, and walls, and furniture of the room may be positively dirty; but, wonderful to relate, the bed was always clean. Only on two or three occasions during my five weeks' travel did I find a single flea, and never anything worse. Many a time did I leave an inn of a morning, with regret that the exigencies of pedestrian travel required a move onward, instead of sleeping again in so clean a bed; but the regret was misapplied, for at night, wherever that might be, at the grand hotel of the luxurious city, or the humble inn of the canton town, the same cleanliness in the way of sleeping accommodation always prevailed. To the pedestrian, who cannot recruit his energies with a nap on the cushions of a luxurious first-class railway carriage, such an ingredient of comfort will prove inestimable.

The expense of living at the Norman inns varies from six francs a-day in the canton towns to eight francs a-day in the cities, including cider, but exclusive of wine. Wherever the English resort, the prices are higher. I never saw any of my countrymen at a *table d'hôte*, or in the precincts of an inn, without knowing that I should have to pay two or three francs for the pleasure of their company. With regard to wine, this is only served in bottles at two francs, a custom inconvenient to the economical sojourner at an inn for a single day, though otherwise of no importance, as the unfinished bottle will be put by for you. I think the Norman innkeepers are making a great mistake in raising the native prices. At some of the principal resorts for tourists, such as Havre, Caen, and Trouville, the prices are about the same as at first-class hotels in Switzerland. Now Normandy will attract tourists from the beauty of the landscape scenery, the splendour of its church architecture, and the propinquity to our own shores, but the attractions are not sufficiently great to enter into rivalry with Switzerland. Therefore, if visitors to Normandy find the prices there the same as those in Switzerland, they will on another occasion proceed further to the latter and more attractive country, and will recommend their friends to do the same. The *table d'hôte* dinner at the Norman inn, I fancy, has been raised from two francs, the native or commercial price, to three francs, beds from one franc, or one franc and a-half, to two francs, and other things in like proportion. The proprietor of the Hôtel du Nord at Granville, one of the best inns in Normandy, though his establishment is much frequented, has, I think, acted most wisely in not raising his prices. You can live there comfortably for eight francs a-day, exclusive of wine, and join both the *tables d'hôte*. Though there is no dishonesty in raising prices, yet I believe the rule adopted by the proprietor of the Hôtel du Nord would be found to constitute the best policy.

The company at the Norman inns consists almost exclusively of commercial gentlemen. When you pass beyond the tourist route, a lady will very rarely form one of the company. Here and there a commercial gentleman will be met travelling with his wife, or a French advocate will appear with a lady who passes as such, but, as a general rule, female society will not be found at the country inns. This, no doubt, is a great disadvantage of travel in the country. The commercial gentlemen I invariably found courteous and obliging in their manners, and ready to enter into conversation. Of course when, as was usually the case, several of them were at the *table d'hôte* dinner, a good deal of shop talk went on among themselves, especially at the small inns where the landlord did not preside, and thus introduce and encourage general topics. I may here observe that at the larger inns the host dines with his customers, sitting near the centre of the table, where there is a large space covered with oilcloth, on which the dishes are placed, to be carved by the master, and then distributed to the guests by the waiters. But at the small country inns the dinner will be brought in by a waiting-maid, and the landlord's place taken by the guest who has been longest in the house, or possesses some kind of accidental superiority, such as age or willingness to serve others. I was always well attended to, by whoever presided, and never had occasion to complain of any incivility or inadvertence. Indeed, there is so little travelling away from the main tourist routes, that were it not for these commercial gentlemen in these out-of-the-way localities, inns would scarcely exist where a traveller for pleasure could stop at with any comfort. A word from one of these gentlemen, as I had frequently occasion to observe, went a long way with the serving-maid. She knew well it must be remembered and acted upon, or loss of custom to the house would be the result, for he who addressed her was not a casual traveller like myself, who would never probably come this way again, but one who periodically appears here, and who would, if ill-treated, put up at the other inn in the place, or failing that at some adjoining town.

The way in which the commercial gentlemen meet one another was worthy of commendation. Two of these who encountered at an inn would take off their hats in the most formal manner, and then, after conversation of the most friendly description, they would part in a similar way, as much as to convey the meaning that though they had thus met, no further acquaintance than existed before need necessarily be considered to have arisen between them.

Indeed, in this matter of bowing we might well borrow a lesson from our continental neighbours. It may seem a small point to dwell upon, but much of the happiness and misery of life is made up of trifles. In England the system of bowing in vogue among acquaintances and friends, who pass each other in the streets and public places without speaking, is simply barbarous and absurd. The inclination of the head and movement of the lips, or, when audible, "How do?" or "How do you do?" or "How do you do, Brown?"—such is the unmeaning practice of salutation prevalent among us. How graceful in comparison is the continental mode of taking off the hat! How much more friendliness does it convey with less effort! It would even be better to follow the custom of the country people, who in saluting simply give one another's name: for instance, "Brown," "Jones." If the practice of taking off the hat were instituted among us, then how pleasant in summer would an extensive acquaintance prove. Fancy, on a hot July day, the comfort of removing the hat every fifty yards or so. How slowly and high you would raise it, how long in bringing it down, in deference to your friend. Or one might, in imitation of Theodore Hook, who took wine with imaginary guests, take off the hat to some supposed friend on the other side of the street. At present, except in the case of a peer, a bishop, or a judge, and ladies, custom forbids the removing of the hat, as it would imply inferiority. Where, indeed, ladies with whom you are not acquainted are in the company of your friend, you may, strictly speaking, take off the hat; but then, I am afraid, you incur the suspicion of having recently worked up some book on etiquette. Perhaps tuft-hunters, instead of being influenced by those unworthy motives which are attributed to them by persons who are unable to achieve a like success, really have in view, in making acquaintances above their own grade in life, the privilege and luxury of being able, consistently with their own dignity, to remove the hat.

One great institution of the Norman city or town is the cafés. These abound everywhere, and many are elegantly and even tastefully fitted up. I have frequently seen and entered, in a canton town, a café of considerable size, and very well furnished. They are attended by all classes, even by labourers in blouses. What is usually taken is a small cup of black coffee, with plenty of sugar, but no milk. Indeed, *café au lait* is difficult to obtain. I asked for it on several occasions; but, being met by excuses, such as the milk was sour, or they would send for it, or it would take time to get ready, that at last I did what I should recommend the reader to do: namely, to follow, in this respect, the custom of the country.

I saw scarcely any drunkenness about. Indeed, I only actually remember three instances: one that of the drunken landlord I have referred to in the course of my travels; another on the road from Vire, in a village, where a crowd was collecting round two drunken men, who were about to fight in a field. The third instance was the most painful of all. It was that of a fine, gentlemanly-looking young man at Alençon. I saw him first in the morning at the café where I had my breakfast, drinking brandy. I saw him again in the evening at the café where I had my coffee, still drinking brandy. He entered with difficulty, but did not forget to raise his cap with becoming dignity. It was evident that the dreadful vice was gaining ground and enclosing him in its fatal folds. He looks intelligent and capable of good work; but as it is, the brain is gradually becoming misty and the mind obscure. I attribute the general prevalence of sobriety in Normandy to the existence of cafés. These not only assuage the thirst by the gentle stimulant of coffee, but they also afford luxurious places of resort for the meeting of friends, where they can, for hours of an evening, engage in conversation or play at dominoes, and are not expected to take more for the good of the house than a small cup of coffee. If similar places could be established in London, and the cities and towns of England, the practical result might be a considerable diminution of drunkenness.

The Normans in manners very much resemble the English. They are unpolished or uncouth, and sometimes seemingly rude in conduct. I was particularly struck with this similarity on many occasions, on first entering a country inn. I was received with coldness and hesitation, and sometimes there would appear to be a doubt even whether I should obtain accommodation. Many times did I feel inclined to follow suit, and abruptly to leave the house without word or comment. But I found, on experience, that such conduct was mere fringe, as it were—only the outward covering, which soon disappeared. In the course of half an hour the real friendliness of the people shone forth, as if from a cloud, and everything appeared light and genial. Such a meal as could be procured was soon forthcoming, and I became satisfied I had fallen into good hands. The peasantry, for the most part, displayed the same roughness of manner, though after the ice was broken, and a little conversation ensued, they became civil enough. As to the gentry, I saw very little of them. They rarely appear at the inns for any purpose. There occasionally passed me a grand carriage, drawn by two horses, and with two servants with white-trimmed liveries. The persons inside were fashionably dressed, and the ladies looked elegant and refined. Leading up from the roadside, too, ever and anon, there was a broad road, straight, and lined with tall poplar trees, and at its termination a large white-looking house. These were the residences of the nobility and gentry of Normandy; but I saw nothing of the interior of any of such houses, nor did I become acquainted with the mode of life of the inhabitants thereof.

A good deal of flax is grown in Normandy, and many of the villages, therefore, assume quite a manufacturing appearance. You see, as you pass, through the open doorways, women and girls hard at work spinning the flax; and the jingle of the numerous wheels of the hand-machines going round falls on the ear of the traveller as he passes onward. Sometimes, also, will be seen, on a village green, men playing at bowls, as in England. I noticed with strange interest that the peasantry, driving horses and cattle along the roads, would use those ejaculatory expressions which I was accustomed to hear as a boy in my own native village, and which I could not express in words, because they are not to be found in any dictionary or written language. Can it be that these strange words are corruptions from the old Norman tongue, which tradition has handed down from mouth to mouth during the centuries which have elapsed since the Conquest? Perhaps so.

The cottages of the peasant class are very

well built, and neat and comfortable. A general air of prosperity presents itself in the villages, and beggars are rarely encountered anywhere.

I have reserved to the last one topic of interest, not because I do not attach sufficient importance to it, but by reason of the difficulty and extreme delicacy of the subject. I allude to the personal appearance of the Normans. The men are a fine race, of muscular proportions, and often of handsome bearing and appearance. The women are well made, tall for the most part, and of good proportions. Those at the little islet of Mont St. Michel are quite of Amazon size. Whether this be owing to the sea-air and healthiness of the locality, or the race be one of some foreign extraction, I don't know; I only chronicle the fact. But as regards the beauty of the women, herein I think there has been great exaggeration on the part of travellers in Normandy. Very rarely I saw a pretty woman; but it occurred to me, on my return home, that frequently during a single walk in London, I observed more pretty girls than I saw during the whole of my travels in Normandy. No doubt an Englishman is not altogether a competent judge of French beauty. There is something angular and masculine about the best-formed French female countenance which is not altogether pleasing to the English eye. It must be borne in mind, also, that different races have different ideas of female beauty. Perhaps it was so designed by nature, in order to keep the races apart; or else how comes it to pass, that with the constant intercourse which now for so many years has taken place between the different continental nations, there should be so few intermarriages amongst them? How rare it is to meet in England a husband and wife natives of different countries.

There is another reason why the beauty of the Norman women is not so apparent to the English eye. They don't know how to dress properly. I allude now to the peasant class and the grades above them, and not to the higher and middle classes, who walk but little about the towns or villages, and not at all along the roads, and are, therefore, not much open to the observation of the stranger. Many a time, on entering a town or village, particularly on Sundays, I could discern the belle of the place a quarter of a mile off, by the gaudy nature of her dress, before I could distinguish the symmetry of her form or the beauty of her countenance. No doubt, in all countries, handsome men and beautiful women are accustomed to add the aid of art to their natural attractions. Plain people, who really require such additions, are generally the most slovenly in appearance. But still, I think the Norman belle commits a grave error against good taste in the matter of dress. Instead of trusting to her own natural charms in order to gain admirers, she considers them as an excuse for decking herself in all kinds of gorgeous apparel.

CHAPTER XIII.

A road under repair—Maromme—Malaunay—No scenery—Tôtes —Good walking condition—The church at Tôtes—The inn— Reception there—An indigestible dinner—A civil commercial gentleman—Again no scenery—The approach to Dieppe—End of my long journey—My claim to sympathy—Reach Dieppe —Weather-worn—Reception at the Hôtel Victoria—Hôtel d'Angleterre—The church—A querulous American—Castle and shops—General Description of Dieppe—Early to bed—A dream—Process of calling—Leave Dieppe—Fine passage— Party of Germans—About clean linen—English spoken, but not understood—Reach Newhaven—An uncivil gatekeeper— An appropriate resting-place—Reflections on the past—Journey to London.

Monday, October 5th.—I left Rouen this morning. My friendly landlord seemed much interested in the idea of my walking to Dieppe, and he opened his eyes with surprise. I apprehend that such an occurrence is a rare thing among his guests. After leaving the city, I traversed the imperial road. This was undergoing repairs, and altogether in that state which a London street presents when the main sewer is out of order. I had to thread my way along the margin of the road with some discomfort, especially as my boots by this time were nearly worn out.

Shortly I pass through the canton town of Maromme, and afterwards Malaunay and other villages. The country is very flat, and there is no scenery. Towards evening I reach Tôtes, a canton town, twenty-nine kilomètres (or eighteen miles) distant from Rouen, and mid-way between that city and Dieppe. I was now in such good walking condition that I felt almost inclined to proceed to Dieppe this night, and step at once on to the steamer in the early morning; but I was afterwards glad I did not do so, for the rain fell in the night in drenching torrents, and the journey would, therefore, have proved very comfortless.

The church at Tôtes is a modern, or, rather, recent, building, of good size. There are two or three curious old statues, no doubt preserved from the original church. There is an altar at the entrance, with a stone archway or enclosure, very fine, though apparently new.

I entered the small inn here, and asked the

landlady, a pretty, middle-aged woman, for a bed-room. Both she and her husband, a stout, burly-looking man, were so curt and uncivil at first, that I felt disposed to leave the place; but this seemed the only decent inn in the town, so I felt constrained to remain. Presently, however, the manner of the good people improved a little, and my hostess showed me to a rough, ill-furnished room. On coming down-stairs, I took my seat by the fire, and just then one of the children of the house, a little girl, entered, and gave me such a pretty courtesy that I at once forgave any rudeness—probably unintentional—on the part of her parents. After a-while, the good woman put a duck on a spit to roast before the fire, and there I was watching its progress. On asking for something to eat, which I had not yet done, the landlady said I should have that, pointing to the duck. When this was roasted, it was taken into an inner room, and I was shown the way there by my hostess. Here a clean table-cloth was laid, and all the adjuncts for dinner, without a word from me. I then perceived that the manner on entering was but fringe, and that both landlord and landlady were really anxious to do all in their power to accommodate the stranger. But the duck proved not well done, and some *vin ordinaire* I ordered was execrable. I should have fared better, probably, with the humble and more digestible food then being partaken of by the host and hostess at supper before the kitchen fire. However, hunger and thirst must be appeased, so I ate a great part of the raw duck, and drank the wine, though at the expense of sickness in the night. There is a South African proverb to the effect that a pedestrian can eat anything. I have found it true sometimes, but not always. Altogether, I was sorry that my experience at the last Norman country inn I stopped at should turn out so unsatisfactory.

Tuesday, Oct. 6th.—After breakfast this morning I sought out my hostess, who was busily engaged over her household work, and paid my reckoning. Just as I was on the threshold, a commercial gentleman, well-dressed and pleasant-looking, drove up, with the horse's head turned in the direction of Rouen. He at once asked the landlady in which direction the stranger was going, evidently with the intention of giving me a lift had I been proceeding to

Rouen, and civilly meaning, as I might not have heard, not to offer a seat which I might not be able to accept. But as it was, my hostess, who knew my destination, declined for me. This morning I walked from Tôtes to Dieppe, twenty-nine kilomètres (or eighteen miles). The country, however, is again flat, and there is no scenery; but the rain in the night had made the road very soft and pleasant for walking.

It was a bright morning. I approach Dieppe over the brow of a gentle hill. Before me lies the town, nestled in the valley beneath, with the sea smooth, with the exception of a slight ripple, beyond, with here and there a small sailing vessel floating rather than moving about. I could not help congratulating myself on thus reaching safely the end of my long, self-imposed journey of five hundred miles through Normandy. There was a peculiar sensation of relief in the idea of arriving at the goal where I would be, a feeling that I had accomplished something; not anything, indeed, dangerous, or likely to be fatal, but still something requiring time, perseverance, strength, toil, weariness, fasting, though not unalloyed with pleasure and happiness.

The reader, perhaps, may be thinking that I am entitled to no sympathy in the indulgence of these feelings; that the task was self-imposed, the tour a holiday project, which need not have been undertaken; and that it would be my own fault had the journey proved disastrous or unfortunate.

To such comments I answer, is not nearly all we take in hand or attempt, in the journey through life, in some sense or other our own fault? One man marries and becomes, as the phrase is, burdened with a large family, which entitles him to the sympathy of his relatives and friends. Is not that *his* fault? Another, in middle age, finds himself alone, without domestic help and sympathy. Is not that *his* fault? Has he not, in the bloom and pride of early manhood, passed by many a beautiful and accomplished girl, who would have been proud to minister to his comfort and make a happy home? One, from motives of self-interest or gain, enters the church: the round of services proves monotonous, his teaching without efficacy, and his example hurtful. Is not that *his* fault? Another supposes himself to possess the gift of healing, and finds that he has made a mistake. Listless and agitated, he goes his slowly decreasing rounds, inspiring no confidence among his patients because he has none himself. Is not that *his* fault? One enters the army, for which he is physically unfitted, and turns back in the day of battle. Another goes to the bar without the power of speech, and life becomes a spiritless blank. Is not that *his* fault? Or, last and most melancholy of all, one who during the long journey of life, while in health and strength, placed his confidence and trust in the philosophy of the schools, and regarded not the pure and simple teaching handed down to him from his forefathers, now approaches the end of his earthly travels. But he feels no confidence in that wherein he trusted then. It inspires no hope in the future—gives no consolation in the present. His relatives and friends flatter him with expectations of returning to that world from which he feels too well that he has for ever departed. The minister of religion, in charity, holds up the cross, as Moses of old held up the serpent in the wilderness, and bids him look thereon. But it is too late! The eye of faith has become obscured by the learning of this world. He cannot say, in the language of one of the most beautiful of our hymns—

> "I know not, oh, I know not
> What joys await us there;
> What majesty of glory,
> What light beyond compare!"

Nor can he realize the idea that—

> "The pastures of the blessed
> Are decked in glorious sheen."

But alone, desolate, and comfortless, he passes through the gates of death, and uncertain of the kind of reception he will meet with in the country beyond. Is not that *his* fault?

I reached Dieppe about three o'clock. I presume I must have presented by this time a somewhat weather-worn, dingy, and poverty-stricken appearance; for, on presenting myself at the entrance of the Hôtel Victoria, on the quay, and asking for a bed-room, the landlady at once said that the charge was three francs, but that, further down, at the Hôtel d'Angleterre, I could obtain a room for two francs. I could not refrain from contrasting this ungracious reception with that I met with at the hotel at Rouen; and it was the more unnecessary, as, curiously enough, I had guessed that would be the charge here. But I am afraid it is so; that wherever the English resort in large numbers, they spend money so lavishly, as rather to throw some suspicion on the solvency of the humble pedestrian. However, after such a reception, the Hôtel Victoria did not seem the place to stop at, and so, though with some inconsistency, I walked on, and had a look at the Hôtel d'Angleterre. This was very small, and presented a forbidding-looking aspect; but it was exactly opposite the steamer which was to leave very early the next morning, and the landlord and landlady, who turned out to be English people, were so civil, that I took a bed-room there, though I was afterwards somewhat chagrined to find that this little inn is a dependence of the Hôtel du Nord et Victoria, itself one establishment, and not two, as the names would denote.

Then I emerged forth to see the town. I saw over the church. It has a fine exterior, with a nave, transept, and choir. I could not quite identify the Lady Chapel, and there is a monument in a chapel in the nave, side aisle to the right, the subject of which is perplexing. There was an American gentleman in the church, who took me to be a Frenchman, and so addressed some remark about this monument. Finding out his mistake, with singular bad taste he commenced very volubly complaining of the bad manners of the English. He gave as an instance, going to a bank in the city to get a bill cashed, and finding the clerk there very uncivil. "In what way?" asked I. "Why," said he, "he did not treat me like a gentleman." "Did you obtain payment of the cheque?" "Oh, yes; but the clerk said nothing; now in America we should have spoken." I felt amused at this grievance, insomuch as most of us are so treated at our bankers, and do not complain, but rather like the absence of ceremony than otherwise. I was annoyed afterwards, thinking whether I ought to have resented this reflection on my own country, but the American spoke so innocently as if not designing any offence; and then, as Lord Bacon says that you may praise the class to which you belong without egotism, so I presume you may hear blame of your country without being called upon to view it in a personal light.

I observed the castle on the West Cliff,

which looks a fine object in the distance. There are two or three shops in the main-street, containing many articles finely worked in ivory. Dieppe looks very well from the sea-side; but it has a shingly beach, and does not come up to one's idea of a good watering-place.

Dieppe is the chief place of the arrondissement. It presents itself to the visitor under two different aspects; one, to a very great many, as a seaport town, at which they arrive or from which they embark with different sensations of retrospect or expectation as to the pleasure or discomfort of the voyage. To these, as they pass through it on their way to the station, the town seems dull and lifeless. To the other and more select class of visitors, Dieppe appears as one of the most fashionable of the French watering-places, with splendid hotels, good *tables d'hôte*, elegantly-furnished lodgings, fine bathing, fashionable promenades, country excursions, endless varieties of dress, and all the accompaniments of fashion. However, the season, though gay, is short. The cold soon sets in here, and sends the fair visitors to warmer climes. As I lounge by the sea-shore, I see little to betoken the place in its life and spirit. Two or three ladies fashionably dressed are walking about, but they seem out of their element. The dinner-bells ring at the grand hotels, but, from the absence of lights in the rooms, to summon but a few solitary guests from their toilet to the repast. A kind of desolation prevails which makes the heart sad, from the contrast, at least, which the stranger supposes it presents at other times.

For myself, I have some dinner at a restaurant, and retire to bed early, after giving directions to my civil landlord to call me in time for the steamer in the morning.

Wednesday, Oct. 7th.—I woke to find it too early to get up, and then to sleep again, when I dreamt a dream which, though relating to a matter of no great importance, by a strange coincidence, turned out, on my arrival home, to be strictly true. Then I woke again to hear the mode by which my landlord himself was being called. A man outside was ringing and shaking the doors, enough to disturb the whole household. At length the landlord responded to the call, and there was silence. I was speculating who called the man outside, and who him, and so on; but, perhaps, the solution is, that the caller is some one connected with the steamer. At any rate, one great advantage, I presume, appertaining to this little inn on the quay, is the certainty of being awoke in time for the steamer, which, depending on the tide, frequently leaves here, as on this morning, at a very untimely hour. Presently the landlord appears to call the already-awakened guest. After the loud noises required to rouse himself, he must have considered it a mere formality.

The steamer left Dieppe this morning at twenty minutes past three o'clock. It was a fine passage, but nevertheless I was sick. There was a party of Germans on board, who made themselves very agreeable. They consisted of two or three young men and a young lady, a pretty girl, and animated. She was well dressed, but on raising or showing her attire, the linen did not appear to be clean. This is a mistake which the German girls almost invariably fall into, so far, at least, as they have come under my own limited observation. Scrupulous cleanliness is one of the best aids to beauty; indeed, without it the charm will often fail of effect. The production by a pretty girl, in the course of the dance, of a soiled pocket-handkerchief, will sometimes for ever destroy the illusion in the mind of the budding admirer. So strangely are we constituted, that "trifles light as air" have a weighty effect. Shakspeare has a fine touch of nature, when, in the rehearsal of the play in the "Midsummer Night's Dream," he makes Bottom give the direction—"In any case, let Thisby have clean linen."

These Germans spoke English pretty well; but I was amused to find that understanding it was quite another matter. One of the young men asked a sailor on board, "When shall we arrive?" The time was stated, and I noted it down in my mind. After an hour or two he asked me the same question, "When shall we arrive?" I said such an hour, remarking that I had the information from the sailor he spoke to some time ago. "Yes," he replied, smiling, "I remember very well putting the question, but I had no idea whatever what the answer was."

We reached Newhaven at half-past nine o'clock. Not feeling well, and having had no breakfast, I determined to proceed to London by a later train. I therefore shouldered my knapsack, and walked along the river's bank until I came to the bridge, which I crossed, and there encountered the gatekeeper, with bag strapped to his side, who demanded the customary penny. I handed a small silver coin for change, which was certainly somewhat defaced. He said, "I don't like the look on't; have he got another?" I then took the coin back and gave him another, which, curiously enough, was about in the same predicament. But this he looked at sullenly, and gave me the change without any remark. After I had passed, I overheard him say to a neighbour who came up, "Well, that 'ere be a queer customer to deal with;" though what there was queer in my conduct I could not comprehend. But I am disagreeably reminded by this petty incident that I have quitted the shores of polite France, and am now again in England, where small discourtesies such as these prevail so much—discourtesies which add so much to the discomfort of life.

I saunter on, and see before me a neat little inn, bearing the designation, "A la Descente de Louis Philippe en 1848." This struck me at once as an appropriate resting-place after my travels in Normandy, and therefore I enter the inn, take my seat in the bar-parlour, and order some breakfast, which is soon brought. I am alone at first, but presently there comes a foreman of carpenters, who has a pint of ale, which he says he takes every morning of his life at this time. A good customer certainly—quite a small annuity for the landlord. He seems strong and well, so this moderate allowance no doubt does him good. Then enters a very young man, a sea captain, who seems to know something of the other. He speaks with what seems to me great *sang froid* of sleeping on board his schooner in the bay, which, he says, was rocking about a good deal in the night, but merely alluding to the circumstance not as one of discomfort, but indicating squally weather. Probably he sleeps as soundly on board this rocking schooner as when a baby in the cradle in some quiet cottage; for it is apparent to me that this very young man has risen from an inferior position. He takes up the "Shipping Gazette," and sees with pleasure that his brother, also a captain, has arrived with his ship at some distant port. A successful family!

However, for my part, I wander back to fifteen years ago, to the ever memorable year

1848. I am again a youth, on the green sward, big with the importance of the staff and white ribbon of the special constable. Here, there, and around me, are a goodly array of some hundreds of men, young, middle-aged, and old, ready and willing to do battle in the cause of right, according to their strength. Where is that fine, tall man, the captain of my own little band of comrades, who afterwards sent a polite note requesting me to come and hear Sir George Grey's letter read out, thanking us for our services? Where the place and room where, with emphasis and pleasure, he read out such letter? I have quite forgotten, as also his very name. I used to pass him occasionally in the street with an air of recognition; but is he dead now, or has he faded gradually from memory beneath the shadows of advancing years? I know not. And where is the second captain of that eventful day, the one we chose when the first went to an institution in the neighbourhood, from whence we, his men, were to seek him if his services were required, but which, though near enough on an ordinary occasion, would be far indeed in the hour of danger? He was shorter than the other, I remember; but, beyond that, his very name and visage are a blank. Where, again, is that tall, well-made, military-looking young man, born to command, who, impatient of inactivity, marched with his company to Charing Cross, to offer his services to Sir Richard Mayne? Great in advance, and still greater in retreat, as he returns, and states to us that the officer on duty thanked them, but recommended that they should return and guard their own locality.

Fifteen years have passed away. Fifteen years! What a change must have come over that varied crowd since then. Some have obtained dignities and honours which they now enjoy. Others have achieved and passed away from them for ever! Some have attained to moderate success, the fruit of early industry and average talents. Others, though possessed of great abilities, have drawn no prize, but their careers are barren, and leafless, and withered. Some have passed away from the scene of this world's labours while the bloom of youth and the freshness of hope remained, and before they had tasted much of the joy or bitterness of life. Others have lived to realize that their early hopes were but as dreams, and that in the lottery of success they have drawn a blank.

Fifteen years! what a change of feeling must have come over that crowd. What tender ties must have been formed and broken—what friendships severed or made—what enmities appeased or roused—what new ideas and opinions. But all, whether living or dead, are to me as they then were, but shadows of the past.

And I, too—for who is there that in such a retrospect of the past does not form the centre figure in the scene?—I, too; but here comes the waiting-maid, pretty and neat, who eyes me as if the time had come to pay the reckoning. I take the hint, shoulder my knapsack, and proceed to the station. After an interval of waiting, the train starts for London. Nothing worthy of record occurred during the onward journey to town, or, at all events, absorbed with thoughts of the past, I observed nothing. And so it came to pass that, having arrived at London Bridge, I emerge from the carriage and disappear in the crowd.

INDEX.

ALENÇON, 156—161.
Argentan, 92, 93.
Avranches, 114—125.

BARENTON, 145.
Bathing, 27—32.
Bayeux, 70—74.
Beuzeville, 39—43.
Bréhal, 105.
Breteuil, 179.
Briouze, 94.

CAEN,
  the road to, 52—54.
  cleanliness of the beds, 217.
  suburbs of, 55.
  hôtel d'Angleterre, 57—59.
  church of St. Pierre, 61, 62.
  St. Etienne, 62.
  St. Etienne le Vieux, 65.
  Abbaye aux Dames, 66.
  Lycée Impériale, 67.
  old houses, 68.
  quarries, 69.
  hôtel de Victoire, 75.
Caudebec, 188.
Conquest,
  reflections on, 50, 51.
  burying-place of William the Conqueror, 62—65.
Corbon, 49.
Country Inns,
  no beds at, 51, 52.
  how to cure incivility, 167, 168.
  their general aspect, 214, 215.

Couptrain, 151.
Coutances, 103, 104.

DENIS, St., 156.
Dieppe, 238—243.
Distances, 23.
Dogs, 179, 180.
Domfront, 146—148.

ÉCOUCHÉ, 94.
Elbeuf, 188, 189.
Evreux, 181—185.

FALAISE, 81—90.
Flers, 94.

GRAND Couron, 191.
Granville, 108—111.
Guibray, 84.

HAVRE,
  the boat from London to, 4—10.
  hôtel l'Amirauté, 11.
  description of, 11—18.
Hilaire du Harcouet, St., 139—142.
Honfleur, 20, 21.

JAMES, St., 137, 138.
Juvigny, 148—151.

LIBRARIES, remarks on, 161.
Lisieux, 47—49.
Lo, St., 102.
Louviers, 185—188.

INDEX.

MALADRERIE, La, 69.
Malaunay, 232.
Marigny, 103.
Maromme, 232.
Maurice, St., 169.
Ménil Broux, Le, 162.
Mesle-sur-Sarthe, Le, 164.
Monopoly, result of, 163.
Mortagne-sur-Huine, 165-167.
Mortain, 142—144.
Mont St. Michel, 127—134.

NORMANDY,
  books about, 2, 3.
  geography of, 22.
  a country of landscapes, 201.
  the rain-fall, 202, 203.
  village churches, 204.
  desecration of old churches, 205.
  middle-class worshippers, 206.
  public gardens, 207—210.
  modes of travelling, 211.
  passports and money, 212—214.
  cider, 215, 216.
  vin ordinaire, 216.
  expense of living, 218, 219.
  company at the inns, 219—221.
  mode of greeting, 221—223.
  cafés, 223, 224.
  absence of drunkenness, 224, 225.
  manners, 225, 226.
  the gentry, 226, 227.
  flax-spinning, 227.
  rustic expressions, *ib.*
  cottages, 228.
  personal appearance and dress, 228—230.
Norrey, 75.

ORIVAL, 189.

PONT au Baud, 126.
—— Audemer, 43—46.
—— Callant, 113.
—— d'Orson, 135, 136.
—— l'Evêque, 33, 34.
Prez-en-Pail, 153—155.

ROADS, 22.
Rouen, 194—199.

SARTILLY, 112.

TINCHEBRAY, 95.
Torigny, 100, 101.
Tôtes, 232—234.
Travel,
  reflections on, 36—38.
  comments about, 158.
Tribunal, 34—36.
Trouville, 25—27.

VAUDERVILLE, 25.
Verneuil, 169—178.
Vire, 96—98.

WASPS, 80.

THE END.

F. BENTLEY AND CO., PRINTERS, LONDON.

www.ingramcontent.com/pod-product-compliance
Lightning Source LLC
Chambersburg PA
CBHW032142230426
43672CB00011B/2420